First World War
and Army of Occupation
War Diary
France, Belgium and Germany

57 DIVISION
172 Infantry Brigade
Prince of Wales's Volunteers (South Lancashire Regiment)
2/4th Battalion
2 February 1917 - 31 May 1919

WO95/2985/8

The Naval & Military Press Ltd
www.nmarchive.com
Published in association with The National Archives

Published by

The Naval & Military Press Ltd

Unit 10 Ridgewood Industrial Park,

Uckfield, East Sussex,

TN22 5QE England

Tel: +44 (0) 1825 749494

www.naval-military-press.com

www.nmarchive.com

This diary has been reprinted in facsimile from the original. Any imperfections are inevitably reproduced and the quality may fall short of modern type and cartographic standards.

© **Crown Copyright**
Images reproduced by permission of The National Archives, London, England, 2015.

Contents

Document type	Place/Title	Date From	Date To
Heading	WO95/2985/8 57 div 172 Inf Brig 2/4 5th Lancs regt 1917 Feb-1919 May		
War Diary	Fely	02/02/1917	31/03/1917
Miscellaneous	List Of Officers Of 2/4th Bn South Lancashire Rgt and dated Of arrival In France	02/02/1917	02/02/1917
War Diary	Erquinghem	01/04/1917	30/04/1917
Heading	War Diary Of 2/4th Bn South Lancashire Regt. From May 1st 1917		
War Diary		01/05/1917	31/05/1917
Miscellaneous	Table Of Arms Ammunition and Equipment To Be carried		
Miscellaneous	172nd Infantry Brigade Intelligence Summary From 6.0. pm. 7th to 6.0. am. 8th May, 1917, Bios-Grenier-Rue Du Bois Sector	08/05/1917	08/05/1917
Miscellaneous	Extract from 172nd Infantry Brigade Summary Of Intelligence		
Miscellaneous	Further Instructions With Reference To Operation Orders No.13 Of 130617	13/06/1917	13/06/1917
Operation(al) Order(s)	Operation Order No. 6 By Major R.J. Chorley, Commanding 2/4th Bn South Lancashire Regt.	20/05/1917	20/05/1917
Miscellaneous	Appendix "E"	21/05/1917	21/05/1917
Miscellaneous	2/4th Bn South Lancashire Rgt. Appendix F.	31/05/1917	31/05/1917
Heading	War Diary Of 2/4th South Lancashire Regt. From June 1st 1917 To June 30th 1917		
War Diary		01/06/1917	30/06/1917
Miscellaneous	172nd Infantry Brigade Appendix 4	10/06/1917	10/06/1917
Operation(al) Order(s)	Operation Order No. 13 By Lt. Col. T.H.S. Marchant, Commanding 2/4th Bn South Lancashire Regiment	13/06/1917	13/06/1917
Miscellaneous	Programme Of Action Of Medium Trench Mortars On The Brigade Sector Up To The 15th Inst.		
Miscellaneous	Reports On Silent Raid Carried Out By 2/4th Battalion South Lancashire Regiment, On The Night Of June 15th, 16th ,1917		
Miscellaneous	Detail Of Parties		
War Diary	Rue Marle Area	01/07/1917	09/07/1917
War Diary	Rue du Bois Sub Sector	10/07/1917	18/07/1917
War Diary	Rest Billets Rue Marle Area	19/07/1917	23/07/1917
War Diary	Erquingham	23/07/1917	25/07/1917
War Diary	Rue De Bois Sub Sector	26/07/1917	28/07/1917
Miscellaneous	Nominal Roll Of Officers		
War Diary	Rue De Bois Sub Sector	28/07/1917	04/08/1917
War Diary	Erquingham	09/08/1917	11/08/1917
War Diary	Rue De Bois Sub Sector	12/08/1917	20/08/1917
War Diary	Rest Billets Erquingham	20/08/1917	28/08/1917
War Diary	Rue De Bois Sub Sector	28/08/1917	31/08/1917
Miscellaneous	Appendix "K" Extract From 57th Divisional Routine Orders	09/08/1917	09/08/1917
Miscellaneous	Extract From 57th Divisional Routine Orders	18/08/1917	18/08/1917
Miscellaneous	Extract From 57th Divisional Routine Orders	13/08/1917	13/08/1917
Miscellaneous	Headquarters		

Heading	War Diary 2/4th S Lancs Regt Vol 8		
War Diary	Rue De Bois Sub Sector	01/09/1917	05/09/1917
War Diary	Rest Billets Erquingham	07/09/1917	11/09/1917
War Diary	Rue De Bois Sub Sector	13/09/1917	17/09/1917
War Diary	Bellerive	19/09/1917	19/09/1917
War Diary	Palfart	20/09/1917	20/09/1917
War Diary	Livossart (Training Area)	20/09/1917	30/09/1917
Miscellaneous	2/4th Bn South Lancashire Rgt.		
War Diary	Livossart	04/10/1917	18/10/1917
War Diary	Campagne	19/10/1917	19/10/1917
War Diary	Proven	23/10/1917	24/10/1917
War Diary	Elverdinghe	26/10/1917	31/10/1917
Miscellaneous	2/4th Bn South Lancashire Regiment		
War Diary	Elverdinghe	02/11/1917	02/11/1917
War Diary	Pilkem	03/11/1917	03/11/1917
War Diary	Langemarck	04/11/1917	07/11/1917
War Diary	Boesinghe	08/11/1917	08/11/1917
War Diary	Audruicq	09/11/1917	09/11/1917
War Diary	Recques	13/11/1917	30/11/1917
Miscellaneous	2/4th Bn South Lancashire Rgt.		
Map	Dispositions Of M Battn 061117		
Miscellaneous	Message Pad		
War Diary	Recques	01/12/1917	07/12/1917
War Diary	Wylder	13/12/1917	17/12/1917
War Diary	Elverdinghe	18/12/1917	31/12/1917
War Diary	Houlthourst Forest Sector	02/01/1918	02/01/1918
War Diary	Menegate Camp	04/01/1918	12/01/1918
War Diary	Armentieres	13/01/1918	17/01/1918
War Diary	Epinette Sector	18/01/1918	21/01/1918
War Diary	Menegate Camp	22/01/1918	25/01/1918
War Diary	Epinette Sector	27/01/1918	30/01/1918
War Diary	Erquinghem	31/01/1918	31/01/1918
War Diary	Pont Nieppe	02/02/1918	02/02/1918
War Diary	Epinette Sector	05/02/1918	06/02/1918
War Diary	Waterlands Camp	08/02/1918	08/02/1918
War Diary	Pont Nieppe	04/02/1918	04/02/1918
War Diary	Waterlands Camp	09/02/1918	10/02/1918
War Diary	Erquinghem	11/02/1918	14/02/1918
War Diary	Estaires	15/02/1918	19/03/1918
War Diary	Cordonnerie Sector	20/03/1918	24/03/1918
War Diary	Rue Biache	26/03/1918	30/03/1918
War Diary	Neuf Berquin	31/03/1918	31/03/1918
Operation(al) Order(s)	Operation Order No. 27 By Lieut. Colonel T.H.S. Marchant Commanding 2/4 Bn South Lancashire Rgt	06/02/1918	06/02/1918
Miscellaneous	2/4th Bn South Lancashire Regt.		
Miscellaneous	Supplement To 57th Divisional Intelligence Summary No C 13 of 30th December 1917		
Miscellaneous	Brigade Orders By Brigadier General G. Paynter D.S.O. Commanding 172nd Infantry Brigade	31/12/1917	31/12/1917
Miscellaneous	Extract From Divisional Routine Orders By Major-General R.W.S Barnes C.B. D.S.O. Commanding 57th Division	12/01/1918	12/01/1918
Miscellaneous	Extract From Divisional Routine Orders By Major-General R.W.S. Barnes, C.B. D.S.O. Commanding 57th Division	17/01/1918	17/01/1918

Miscellaneous	Nominal Roll Of Officers 2/4th Bn South Lancashire Regiment		
Miscellaneous	2/4th Bn South Lancashire Regiment		
War Diary	Henu	05/05/1918	05/05/1918
War Diary	Coigneux	06/05/1918	07/05/1918
War Diary	Gommecourt	06/05/1918	26/05/1918
War Diary	Coigneux	17/05/1918	29/05/1918
War Diary	Biez Wood	31/05/1918	31/05/1918
Operation(al) Order(s)	Operation Order No. 40 By Lieut Colonel T.H.S. Marchant Commanding 2/4th Bn. South Lancashire Regiment		
Operation(al) Order(s)	Operation Order No. 40 By Lieut. Colonel T.H.S. Marchant Commanding		
Miscellaneous	2/4th Bn South Lancashire Regiment		
Miscellaneous	Inspection Of Battalions Major-General R.W.S Barnes, C.B., D.S.O. Commanding 57th Division		
Miscellaneous	Extract From 172nd Infantry Brigade Intelligence Summary, 24 Hours Ended 6 a.m. 24th March 1918		
Miscellaneous	O.C. 2/4th Bn S. Ban Rgt.	28/03/1918	28/03/1918
War Diary	Biez Wood	01/06/1918	07/06/1918
War Diary	Reserve Bn. Pigeon Wood Area	08/06/1918	14/06/1918
War Diary	Chateau De La Haie	17/06/1918	23/06/1918
War Diary	Gommecourt	27/06/1918	30/06/1918
Miscellaneous	2/4th Bn South Lancashire Regiment		
War Diary	Gommecourt Wood	01/07/1918	02/07/1918
War Diary	St Leger	05/07/1918	29/07/1918
War Diary	Som Brin	30/07/1918	30/07/1918
War Diary	St. Aubyn	31/07/1918	31/07/1918
Miscellaneous	A Form Messages And Signals.		
Heading	2/4 South Lancashire Regiment		
Miscellaneous	The Officer Commanding, 2/4th Bn. South Lancashire Regt.	05/09/1918	05/09/1918
War Diary	Arras	01/08/1918	01/08/1918
War Diary	Fampoux Sector	03/08/1918	29/08/1918
War Diary	Henin	29/08/1918	29/08/1918
War Diary	Hindenburg Line	31/08/1918	01/09/1918
War Diary	Heninel Fontaine	02/09/1918	02/09/1918
War Diary	Riencourt	03/09/1918	03/09/1918
War Diary	Croisilles	07/09/1918	08/09/1918
War Diary	Inchy En Artois	09/09/1918	16/09/1918
War Diary	Bullecourt	17/09/1918	17/09/1918
War Diary	Bailleulval	25/09/1918	25/09/1918
War Diary	Laganncourt	27/09/1918	30/09/1918
Miscellaneous	2/4th Bn. South Lancashire Regiment		
Miscellaneous	2/4th Bn. South Lancashire Regt.		
Miscellaneous	Ref.B.M.131.		
Miscellaneous	2/4th Bn. South Lancashire Regiment	01/09/1918	01/09/1918
Map	Cherisy		
Miscellaneous	Reference Sketch On Back		
War Diary	La Folie Wood	01/10/1918	01/10/1918
War Diary	Fontaine-Notre-Dame	02/10/1918	06/10/1918
War Diary	Cambrai	08/10/1918	10/10/1918
War Diary	Moeuvres	12/10/1918	12/10/1918
War Diary	Verquin	14/10/1918	14/10/1918
War Diary	Fromelles	16/10/1918	16/10/1918
War Diary	Radinghem	17/10/1918	17/10/1918

War Diary	Lille	19/10/1918	22/10/1918
War Diary	Honnevain	24/10/1918	27/10/1918
War Diary	Froyennes	28/10/1918	30/10/1918
War Diary	Chereng	31/10/1918	31/10/1918
Miscellaneous	Secret 2/4 Bn South Lancashire	07/10/1918	07/10/1918
Miscellaneous	Nominal Roll Of Officer 2/4 Bn South Lancashire Regt.	23/10/1918	23/10/1918
Miscellaneous	2/4th Bn. South Lancashire Rgt.	15/09/1918	15/09/1918
Miscellaneous	2/4 Bn South Lancashire Rgt.	29/10/1918	29/10/1918
Miscellaneous	2/4th Bn. South Lancashire Regt.		
Miscellaneous	2/4th Bn South Lancashire Regt.	29/10/1918	29/10/1918
Miscellaneous	Notes On Operations carried Out By The 2/4th South lancashire regt On 27th,28th,and 30th Sept 1918 and 8th October 1918	10/10/1918	10/10/1918
Miscellaneous	Normal Roll Of Officers 2/4 Bn South Lancashire Rgt.		
War Diary	Chereng	01/11/1918	01/11/1918
War Diary	Lille	11/11/1918	30/11/1918
Miscellaneous	Notes On Inspection Of 172nd Inf. Bde	14/11/1918	14/11/1918
Miscellaneous	Notice		
Miscellaneous	Nominal Roll Of Officers and Other ranks Of The 2/4th Bn South lancashire regiment who formed The guard Of Honour To marshal foch On 15th November 1918		
Miscellaneous	Honours and Awards	18/11/1918	18/11/1918
Miscellaneous	2/4th Bn South Lancashire Regiment		
War Diary	Fives Lille	03/12/1918	03/12/1918
War Diary	Bois L'Epinoy	04/12/1918	04/12/1918
War Diary	Maroeuil	07/12/1918	31/12/1918
Miscellaneous	Extracts From 172nd Infantry Brigade Intelligence Summary,24 Hours Ending 6 am. 24th March 1918	24/03/1918	24/03/1918
Heading	57th Division 172nd Infantry Brigade War Diary 2/4th Battalion The South Lancashire Regiment April 1918		
War Diary	Neuf Berquin	01/04/1918	01/04/1918
War Diary	(Nieppe Forest Le Parc	03/04/1918	03/04/1918
War Diary	Beaudricourt	04/04/1918	04/04/1918
War Diary	Sombrin	08/04/1918	08/04/1918
War Diary	Marieux	09/04/1918	12/04/1918
War Diary	Warluzel	13/04/1918	13/04/1918
War Diary	Henu	14/04/1918	30/04/1918
Miscellaneous	2/4th Bn South Lancashire Regiment Appendix "D"		
Miscellaneous	Extract From 57 Divisional Routine Orders	31/03/1918	31/03/1918
Miscellaneous	Extract from 57th Divisional Routine Orders d/d	07/04/1918	07/04/1918
Miscellaneous	2/4th Bn South Lancashire Regiment		
War Diary	Maroeuil	04/10/1919	31/10/1919
Miscellaneous	Nominal Roll Of Officers.		
Miscellaneous	Strength On Last return	28/01/1919	28/01/1919
War Diary	Maroeuil	01/02/1919	28/02/1919
Miscellaneous	2/4th Bn South Lancashire Regiment Appendix D		
War Diary	Maroeuil	07/03/1919	30/03/1919
Miscellaneous	2/4th Bn South Lancashire Regiment		
War Diary	Maroeuil	03/04/1919	30/04/1919
Miscellaneous	2/4th Bn South Lancashire Regiment		
Miscellaneous	2/4th Battn. South Lancashire Regt	31/05/1919	31/05/1919
War Diary	Maroeuil	13/05/1919	31/05/1919
Heading	57th Division 172nd Infy Bde 2-5th Bn Sth Lancs Regt 1915 Sep-1916 Feb And Feb-Dec 1917		

WO 95 2985/8

57 Dvn; 172 Inf. Brig.
2/4 5th Lancs Regt.
1917 Feb- 1917 May

Army Form C. 2118.

WAR DIARY
–of–
INTELLIGENCE SUMMARY.
(Erase heading not required.)

Instructions regarding War Diaries and Intelligence Summaries are contained in F.S. Regs., Part II. and the Staff Manual respectively. Title pages will be prepared in manuscript.

Hour, Date, Place		Summary of Events and Information	Remarks and references to Appendices
Feby 2nd	1917	Lieut H F BELL Joined Lts R E GORDON, F.I. JACKSON, D. JACOBS. H. MARSH and 14 other ranks sailed from FOLKESTONE and disembarked at BOULOGNE as advanced party	RJE
14th	6·15 pm	Transport embarked at SOUTHAMPTON under Major WH McCLURE Capt R.P.CARTER, LIEUT C.R.SMITH 2 OR 64 Non ranks 22 horses	RJE
15	midnight	The Bn left FRITH HILL Barracks and entrained from FRIMLEY Sta Strength 31 Officers and 799 O.R. under Command of Lieut Colonel J.H.S.MARCHANT. List of Officers see Appendix A	RJE
15	5 pm	Transport disembarked at HAVRE and proceeded to No 5 Rest Camp	RJE
16	7 am	Bn arrived at FOLKESTONE proceeded to Rest Camp. Lieut and	RJE
	10 am	embarked at FOLKESTONE and arrived at BOULOGNE 11·30 am and	RJE
		proceeded to OSTROHOVE Rest Camp	RJE
17	11 am	Entrained BOULOGNE and arrived at BAILLEUL via HAZEBROCK at 5 pm and proceeded to BORRE Billets in farms at BORRE and HAZEBROCK	RJE
	8 am	Transport entrained at HAVRE	RJE
18	10 am	Transport detrained BAILLEUL and proceeded to BORRE and joined	RJE
19	5·30 am	The Battalion at 5·30 am	RJE
22		Proceeded by march route to OUTTERSTEENE and were billeted in farms	RJE
23		Proceeded by march route to SAILLY sur LYS arriving at 2 pm	RJE
24		Took over line of trenches BOIS GRENIER Sector SHAFTESBURY AVE exclusive to PARK ROW Ave inclusive	Ref Map BOIS GRENIER 36 NW 4 1:10000 RJE
25th to 28th		BOIS GRENIER Sector	RJE

WAR DIARY
or
INTELLIGENCE SUMMARY.

(Erase heading not required.)

Army Form C. 2118.

2/4th S. Lancs.

Hour, Date, Place		Summary of Events and Information	Remarks and references to Appendices
March 1916	4th 11am	Tour of Trenches on attack 4th Infantry the Bn. was relieved by the 2/5 S Lan R. Casualties during tour 2 killed 16 wounded	A.J.S.
	4	Relief commenced at 11am and proceeded to Billets La POLANDERIE	A.J.S
		ERQUINGHEM and remained in Brigade Reserve until March 8th	A.J.S
	8th 4pm	1/2 Batn. relieved 1/2 Bn. 38th AUSTRALIAN Bn in RUE du BOIS Section	A.J.S. Ref 7 Mar 36 NW4 Edition 6D Trenches
	9 7pm	1/2 Batn. relieved 1/2 Bn. 38 AUSTRALIAN Bn on ROE du BOIS Sector occupying from WELLINGTON Ave to LEITH Walk inclusive	A.J.S
	13	Frontage extended on right to PARK ROW Ave exclusive occupying NE work of the RUE du BOIS Sector	A.J.S
	20 7am	Relieved by the 2/5 S Lan R and (accessorily) ½ Bn 2/4 L N Lan R in PO de MARLE in Brigade Reserve the one company which returned in Billets at ERQUINGHEM. 11 November (including withdrawals) Casualties during tour of Trenches 3 K 15L	A.J.S
	26 27.	Lieut M F BELL invaliding to ENGLAND 2nd Lieut J.THWAITES joined for duty from 2/5 L N Lan R	A.J.S A.J.S
	29 4pm	Relieved by the 3/4 Foot Regt and proceeded to the LAUNDRIES, ERQUINGHEM in Divisional Reserve 15 Platoons working in trenches (5 by day 10 by night)	A.J.S
	30	2nd Lieut P.O. PLATT'S joined for duty from 4th Res S Lan R	A.J.S
	31	Strength of Battn. on March 31st 39 Officers 830 other ranks	A.J.S

103

APPENDIX A.

List of Officers of 2/4th Bn South Lancashire Rgt. and dated of arrival in FRANCE.

****

Lieut M.F. Bell.	Landed at BOULOGNE
2nd Lieut K.L. Gordon.	February 2nd, 1917
2nd Lieut F.I. Jackson.	as
2nd Lieut D. Jacobs.	advance party.
2nd Lieut H. Marsh.	
Major W. McClure.	Embarked at SOUTHAMPTON
Captain R.P. Carter.	with Transport February
Lieut C.D. Smith.	14th, 1917, arriving HAVRE, February 15th, 1917.

The following Officers arrived at BOULOGNE with the Battalion on April 16th, 1917.

Lt.Col. T.H.S. Marchant.	In Command. From 13th Hussars.
Major R.J. Chorley.	
Lieut & Adjutant S. Jepson.	1st North Staffs.
Captain J. Glascott.	Machine Gun Corps.
Captain F.H. Preedy.	
Captain R.A. Fox.	
Captain H.F. Sawyer.	
Captain R.B. Fairclough.	
Captain G.S. Burniston.	7th W. Yorks.
Captain A. Thompson.	7th W. Yorks.
Captain B. Milburn.	7th W. Yorks.
Lieut S.T. Quint.	
Lieut C.G. Linnell.	
Hon Lt. & Q.M. F. Brook.	
2nd Lieut J. Brookes.	
2nd Lieut C.E. Clarkson.	
2nd Lieut C.A. Lunghi.	7th Lpool R.
2nd Lieut G.B. Smith.	Northum D. Coy.
2nd Lieut H. Marsh.	4th E. Lancs.
2nd Lieut A.J. Watson.	4th E. Lancs.
2nd Lieut J.R. Semple.	9th Lpool R.
2nd Lieut H.G. Rhodes.	7th Lpool R.
2nd Lieut F. Clegg.	4th (R) S.L.R.
2nd Lieut A.E. Watson.	7th Lpool R.
2nd Lieut A.H. Grant.	3rd S.L.R.
2nd Lieut C.J. Grierson.	5th Lpool R.
2nd Lieut H.L. Stevens.	5th Lpool R.
2nd Lieut E.W. Hodson.	5th Lpool R.
2nd Lieut D.J. Mearns.	5th Lpool R.
Captain W.C.D. Hills.	R.A.M.C.
Captain & Rev. W. Brown.	C of E. (Attached)
Captain & Rev. C.W. Roberts.	R.C.

Lt*S.James

Army Form C. 2118.

WAR DIARY
INTELLIGENCE SUMMARY.
(Erase heading not required.)

Instructions regarding War Diaries and Intelligence Summaries are contained in F.S. Regs., Part II. and the Staff Manual respectively. Title pages will be prepared in manuscript.

104

Hour, Date, Place	Summary of Events and Information	Remarks and references to Appendices
APRIL 1st to 10 1917		
10th/4/14	Before the launches EPOUINGHEN	RJC
	Capt J. GLASCOTT, Lieut C.D. SMITH and Lieut D. JACOBS took part in a raid organized by 172 Bde on enemies trenches which was unsuccessful. Capt J. GLASCOTT was in command of the Raid. 2nd Lieut D. JACOBS was seen to face whilst gallantly leading his men and is reported missing. Lt C.D. SMITH was wounded in the arm after returning from a time with great gallantry to enemies wire to bring in our wounded.	RJC
13		
4 am	The Battn relieved the 2/4 Sheets Regt in the RUE du BOIS Sector and remained on this sector until 21st Casualties during this tour 3 killed 11 wounded (4 shell shock)	RJC
21st	Enemy artillery more active during this period	RJC
10 pm	Relieved by the 2/5 Staff R and proceeded to Billets RUE MARLE Area	RJC
26	2nd Lieut J.W. ANDERSON joined to duty from 3 Bn Staff R (SR)	RJC
16th	2nd Lieut H. MARSH invalided to hospital	RJC
29th	Relieved the 2/5 Staff R on RUE du BOIS SECTOR relief commencing at 9 pm STRENGTH at end of Month APRIL 37 Officers 810 OR RUE du BOIS Sector	RJC

No. 5

Confidential

War Diary

of

2/4th Bn South Lancashire Regt

From May 1st 1917

To May 31st 1917

Vol 4

Army Form C. 2118.

IV

WAR DIARY
of
INTELLIGENCE SUMMARY.
(Erase heading not required.)

Instructions regarding War Diaries and Intelligence Summaries are contained in F. S. Regs., Part II. and the Staff Manual respectively. Title pages will be prepared in manuscript.

Hour, Date, Place	Summary of Events and Information	Remarks and references to Appendices
MAY 1st 1917	RUE du BOIS Sector	RJE
7th	Capt G.S. BURNISTON and 7th W YORKS Regt attached wounded	RJE
6th	and Lieut J. BROOKES wounded	RJE
7th	German anti-aircraft shell exploded on head RUEMARLE in the vicinity of the	RJE
	Q.M. Stores. Casualties 3 O.R.	
Night of 7th 8th 7-40 pm	R.Q.M.S. and 2 O.R. wounded 3 Mules killed and 3 curtain class	RJE
	GAS ALARM See Appendices B. Brigade Intelligence Summary	RJE Appendices B
12.45	NGS	
	ENEMY Bomb Barrage on the vicinity of COWGATE AVENUE and ORCHARD	RJE Appendices B and C
	and attempted a raid our trenches See Appendices B and C	
3:0 pm	Situation Normal Casualties 1 Killed 1 Wounded OR	RJE
	Relieved 6/2/5 S.LAN.R and proceeded to Rest Billets RUEMARLE AREA	RJE
8th	Total Casualties for four days 5 Killed 8 Wounded	RJE
9th	2nd Lieut J.W. ANDERSON evacuated to Hospital Suffering from Concussion	RJE
	DRAFT Received of 62. Other Ranks	RJE
10th 11th	RUE MARLE Area	RJE
13th	2nd Lieut C.H. LONGSHAW and 2nd Lieut A. RITCHIE Joined to duty from	RJE
	4th Reserve Bn S. LAN R	RJE
15th	Lt. Col T.H.S. MARCHANT assumes temporary command of the 172 Inf Bde during	RJE
	the absence of Brig General G. PAYNTER DSO.	
16	Major P.J. CHORLEY DSO and Company of Bn	RJE
	Relieved the 2/5 S.LAN.R in the RUE du BOIS Sub Sector BOIS GRENIER Sector	RJE
	Relief commenced 9-15 pm	
19th	Enemy patrol seen looking over parapet RUE du Bois Salient	Trench Map 36 NW & BOIS GRENIER
20	they disappeared leaving the Gents Scheme Post threw bomb and	RJE
	S.O.R. Experince from Reinforcement Camp wounded	
Night of 20th	Automatic Pistol cone Stud bomb discovered RUE du Bois Salient on Notices enemy	RJE
	patrol was seen on the night of the 19th/20th	RJE

Army Form C. 2118.

V

WAR DIARY
INTELLIGENCE SUMMARY.
(Erase heading not required.)

Instructions regarding War Diaries and Intelligence Summaries are contained in F.S. Regs., Part II. and the Staff Manual respectively. Title pages will be prepared in manuscript.

Hour, Date, Place 1917	Summary of Events and Information	Remarks and references to Appendices
MAY 20th 10.30 pm	Raid on Enemy Trench with the Intention of Capturing prisoner 2/6.30-pm o.c Raid Capt J.GLASCOTT. O.C Attack 2nd Lieut R.B.SMITH. Patrol Leader 2nd Lieut R.RANT and 34.O.R. Raid proved unsuccessful Operation on the see Appendix D Report Appendix E No Casualties	French Map BOIS GRENIER 36 NW 4 squares exclusive 74 PJG Appendix D E
21st	RUE du BOIS Sub Sector BOIS GRENIER Sector	PJG
22	"	Rdo
23	"	PJG
24	" Relieved by the 2/5th Bn S.L.A.N.R. Relief completed 10.10pm 30 men rejoined from Reinforcement Camp	PJG
25.26.27	Proceeded to lest billets RUE MARLE area Casualties during tour of trenches 8.0.R wounded Exceptionally quiet tour of trenches	PJG PJG PJG
28	1st Col T.H.S. MARCHANT relinquished temporary command of 172nd Iny Bde and rejoined Unit	PJG
29	Billets RUE MARLE Area	PJG
30	2nd Lieut D.W. WINSTANLEY joined for duty from 4th Res Bn S. L.A.N.R RUE MARLE Area.	PJG
31st	List of Officers with Bn on 31st MAY attached Total Strength of Bn on 31st MAY 1917 Officers 36 including Col P. Chaplain other Ranks 638 including T.M.B. and all supernumaries	Appendix F PJG

APPENDIX A.

TABLE
of
ARMS, AMMUNITION and EQUIPMENT,
to be carried.

Articles.	Officers	N.C.Os. & MEN.				Remarks
		Assaulting Parties	Covering Parties	Bombers	L.Gunners.	
Revolvers.	1.				1.	
Revolver Ammunition	10rds				10rds	
Rifles.		1.	1.	1 per 2 men.		The numbers of articles in
Bayonets.	1.	1.	1.	1.		these columns
P.H. Helmets.	1	1	1	1	1	are carried by
Whistle	1	1 per N.C.O.				each individual, except where it
Torch.	1					is otherwise
Identification label	1	1	1	1	1	stated.
S.A.A.		1 Bandolier	1 bandolier.		4 drums per gun	
Mills Grenades.	2	1		10	1	
Smoke Bombs.		1				
Bomb Carriers.				1 per 2men.		
Wirecutters		2 per party.				

3 Lewis Guns will be taken.

4. Smoke Candles may be carried by Harding's Party, should the wind be favourable.

APPENDIX B.

C.O.P.Y. 172nd INFANTRY BRIGADE INTELLIGENCE SUMMARY From 6.0.pm.7th to 6.0.am. 8th May, 1917, BOIS-GRENIER - RUE DU BOIS SECTOR.

CONFIDENTIAL - NOT TO BE TAKEN FORWARD OF COY HDQRS.

A. OUR OPERATIONS.
1. ARTILLERY.   Prearranged shoots carried out. Slight retaliation received over right sub-sector during second shoot only.
Our left Battalion called for S.O.S. at 1.20.am. and our artillery replied promptly.

B. ENEMY OPERATIONS.
1.   Gas alarm raised at 7.40.pm. by sector on our left was passed on by us and slight cloud of gas passed over the Subsidiary Line of the RUE DU BOIS sub-sector between 8.30. and 9.30.pm. No casualties.
At 12.45.am. enemy M.Gs. placed a box barrage round front, support and sibsidiary lines in the vicinity of COWGATE AV. and T.M. and shrapnel barrage on front line at I.15.1., I.15.2. and ORCHARD.
This was followed by what appeared to be an attempted raid behind a screen of smoke but our artillery and L.G. fire prevented enemy reaching our trenches.
Casualties 1 killed and 1 wounded.
Normal conditions resumed at 3.0.am. since when all has been quiet.

G.T. Lucy, Captain,
Brigade Major,
172nd Infantry Brigade.

8/5/17.

APPENDIX C.

EXTRACT FROM 172nd INFANTRY BRIGADE SUMMARY
OF INTELLIGENCE.
****

Further report regarding attempted raid on RUE DU BOIS
Sub-sector -   At 1.45. am. enemy opened heavy machine gun,
T.M. and artillery fire on our front line and supports at
I.15.1., I.15.2. and ORCHARD, which was followed soon
after by a cloud of smoke. In the meantime, a red flare was
fired by mistake for a "Very" light by the left Company of
the BOIS GRENIER Sub-sector, to which our artillery replied.
      When the smoke cloud was observed the S.O.S. was signalled
from RUE DU BOIS Sub-sector, and our guns were turned on to
the required area. Our L.T.Ms. also joined in, and heavy L.G
fire was directed into the cloud of smoke. The enemy was
unable to approach our trenches and abandoned his enterprise.
On his firing two green lights, his M.G. fire ceased and
artillery gradually died down until all was quiet at about
3.0.am.
With the exception of one large gap blown in our parapet,
damage to our trenches was slight and only two casualties
were sustained (1 killed and 1 Wounded.
The conduct of our garrison was most satisfactory and the
emergency was dealt with with great coolness and expedition.
From specimens of Machine Gun Bullets found in our trenches
fired by the enemy, it is surmised that they were fired from
old and well used barrels as rifling marks are almost
imperceptible.

APPENDIX C.

CODE WORDS.

Raiding Parties gone out.	-	"Gladys"
Raiding Parties entered	-	"Kate"
Raiding Parties returning	-	"Mary"
Raiding Parties **returned**	-	"Sibyl"
Covering Parties in position	-	"Alice"
All in safely	-	"Victoria"

Enemy opposing strongly	-	"Ernest"
Enemy S.O.S. gone up	-	"Sam"
Enemy barrage down	-	"Bob"
Enemy pressing us hard	-	"Harry"
Artillery assistance required	-	"Archibald"

NOTE:- When referring to any particular party its name should be added to the above code, thus :-

"Enemy opposing Smith's Party strongly"

would read - Ernest Smith.

"Fairclough's Party returned"

would read Sibyl Fairclough

Further Instructions with reference to
Operation Orders No.13 of 13/6/17.

---

1. ZERO HOUR. - will be as under and not as stated in
order XII :-

   LEFT RAID   - 11.0.pm.

   RIGHT RAID - 11.15.pm.

2. VICKERS GUNS. - will fire intermittently all night on
gaps at:- I.16.d.20.38., I.22.a.77.83.
They will also fire usual bursts of fire on
gaps at:- I.22.a.45.65.
         I.21.d.00.75.
         I.22.a.12.40.
         I.21.c.85.53.

   until 10.45.pm., when they will raise their
   elevation continuing their usual bursts on
   the enemy back areas.

ASSEMBLY. - All Parties will be in position by 10.15.pm.
at which hour O.C. Raids will notify Advanced Battalion
Headquarters that all is ready.

(Sgd) J.Thwaites, 2nd Lt. & A/Adjt.
            2/4th Bn South Lancashire Regt.

SECRET.   COPY NO. 4   APPENDIX D.

OPERATION ORDER NO 6.
by
Major R.J. Chorley,
commanding
2/4th Bn South Lancashire Regt.   20/5/17.
****

Reference Map 36.N.W.4.
$\frac{1}{10,000}$

INFORMATION.	There is an Infantry Post at I.21.b.50.20. there are no troops garrisoning trenches on his left in his present front line as far as GERMAN HOUSE, and the nearest post on his RIGHT is at least 150 yards N.
INTENTION.	The Patrol as detailed hereunder will capture this Post, secure an identification and withdraw. Should it not be possible to do this the Assault Patrol, will, by searching his line, secure an identification at any other suitable point before withdrawing.

		Officers.	O.R.
DISTRIBUTION OF TROOPS.	O.C. Raid. - Captain J. Glascott.	1	
	O.C. Attack. - 2nd Lt. Smith.	1	
	Patrol Leader. 2nd Lt. Grant.	1	
ASSAULT PATROL.	2 Officers. (O.C. Attack & Patrol Leader)		
	1 Sergeant.		1
	1 Corporal.		1
	2 O.R.		2
COVERING TROOPS.	RIGHT. - 1 Lance Corporal, 7 O.R.		8
	LEFT. - 1 Lance Corporal, 7 O.R.		8
RESERVES.	O.R.		4
		3	24

ACTION.	Before the Assault Patrol leaves British Front Line, Lt. Smith will post LEFT Covering Troops at I.21.b.50.75. O.C. Raid and Reserve will take up a position in British Front Line I.15.d.30.15. Following these dispositions, which will be completed by 10.30.pm. the Assault Patrol accompanied by RIGHT COVERING Party will move off, and having arrived at I.21.b.30.45. will leave RIGHT Covering Party there, and proceed to carry out the intention of this operation.
EQUIPMENT.	All ranks will wear soft caps, Box Respirator, 2 Bombs, and, as far as possible, Patrol Suits. Officers and N.C.Os. of the Assault Patrol will be armed with revolvers, 24 rounds of ammunition, and whistles, and will carry rope and gags. All other ranks will be armed with rifles and 50 rounds S.A.A.
SPECIAL INSTRUCTIONS.	All will remove any papers or marks of identification, and will wear a label tied round their necks with Rank, Name and Initials, and Religion only.
SIGNALS.	Hissing will be used to attract attention between groups. The word 'ROYAL' will be used as password during operations. Whistles will only be used in case of great emergency, and then to call for assistance and support from Covering troops only.
	Telephonic communication will be established between O.C. Raid and H.F.2.
	The Battalion M.O. will remain on duty until O.C. Raid has reported All Clear to him.

P.T.O.

Reports will be rendered verbally to the Battalion immediately the operation is completed, and written reports for transmission to Brigade by Stand-To a.m. 21/5/17.

                              Lieut & Adjutant,
            2/4th Bn South Lancashire Regiment.

Issued to:-

Copy No.1. Brigade H.Q.
     No.2. O.C. Raid.
     No.3. File.
     No.4. War Diary.
     No.5. " "

Appendix "E"

REPORT.

From:- 2nd Lieut Grant
To:-   Captain Glascott.   21/5/17.

Sir,
        I beg to report that the Patrol and Right Covering Party
left our parapet about 10.30.p.m. at the Right post of the
Centre Company. After fixing the Covering Party at approx:
I.21.b.30.45. the Patrol worked along the German wire to the left.
The gap located on the night of the 17/18th was not to be found,
but a way was made through the Bosche wire at about I.21.b.60.20.
There are four lines of wire here but there are gaps in various
parts of each row, and running from the row nearest to the parapet and up to the parapet at about Thirty yards distance are
vertical lines of wire. When getting through the wire a working
party was heard out in front of the parapet and we attempted to
get to close quarters with them. We managed to get within about
thirty yards of them but after that it was found impossible to
get any closer owing to the ground in front being quite open and
also covered with trip wires. Any shell holes that there were
were also well wired. The party appeared to be working on the
parapet and we estimated that there were about half a dozen of
them. We lay up close to them to see if by any chance they would
come nearer with their work and so get within striking distance
but dawn was approaching with no sign of them moving and our
party was forced to withdraw. If we could have laid out a Bosche
there would have been great difficulty in getting him through the
wire, although identification could no doubt be established by
means of shoulder straps &c.

                            Sgd.........G.B. Smith. 2nd Lt.
                                 Alec H. Grant. 2ndLt.

FROM:- Captain J. Glascott.
             2/4th Bn South Lancashire Rgt.
TO:-   Headquarters,
             172nd Infantry Brigade.

        Herewith report from O.C. Assault. The Assault party did
not return until 3.30.am. and have not reported that they were
subject to rifle and M.G. fire, which I myself witnessed.
        The officers of the party have a proposition to offer to
tackle this raid, but with the exception of themselves and Sgt
Price they say the men have not sufficient experience for this
sort of a job.
        The officers complain that they have a lot of difficulty
of locating their position in the very extensive system of
enemy wire.

5.30.am.   Sgd.......J. Glascott. Captain,
21/5/17.   2/4th Bn South Lancashire Rgt.

31st May, 1917.   2/4th Bn South Lancashire Rgt.   APPENDIX F.

HEADQUARTERS.

Commanding Officer	Lt.Col. T.H.S. Marchant.	17th. Hussars.
Second in Command	Major R.J. Chorley.	
Adjutant	Lieut S. Jepson.	1st N.Staff
Quarter Master	2nd Lieut A.J. Watson.	4th(R)E.Lan
Intelligence Officer	2nd Lieut F.I. Jackson.	Rgt
Transport Officer	Captain R.P. Carter.	
Pioneer & Assist: Adj:		
Medical Officer	Captain W.C.D. Hills.	R.A.M.C.T.
Signalling Officer	2nd Lieut C.E. Clarkson.	
Lewis Gun Officer	2nd Lieut J. Thwaites.	2/5 L.N.L.

A. Company.

Captain J. Glascott.	4th S.R. N. Staffs R.
Captain R.B. Fairclough.	
Lieut S.T. Quint.	
2nd Lieut C.A. Lunghi.	7th (R) Lpool R.
2nd Lieut C.J. Grierson.	5th(R) Lpool R.
2nd Lieut D.W. Winstanley.	

B. Company.

Captain A. Thompson.	7th (R) W. Yorks R.
2nd Lieut G.B. Smith.	Northum: Div: Cyclist Coy.
2nd Lieut H.G. Rhodes.	7th (R) Lpool R.
2nd Lieut H.L. Stevens.	5th (R) Lpool R.
2nd Lieut A. Ritchie.	

C. Company.

Major Wm McClure.	
Lieut C.G. Linnell.	
2nd Lieut F. Clegg.	
2nd Lieut E.W. Hodson.	5th (R) Lpool R.
2nd Lieut C.H. Longshaw.	

D. Company.

Captain R.A. Fox.	
Captain B. Milburn.	7th (R) W.Yorks R.
2nd Lieut K.L. Gordon.	
2nd Lieut A.E. Watson.	7th (R) Lpool R.
2nd Lieut A.H. Grant.	3rd S.R. S.Lan R.
2nd Lieut D.J. Mearns.	5th (R) Lpool R.

Commandant 57th Div:Reinforcement Camp.....Hon Lt. & Q.M. F. Brook.
    Brigade Bombing Officer........Captain H.S. Sawyer.
    172nd Inf.Bde. Pioneer Coy....2nd Lieut P.O. Platts. 4th (R) S.Lan R.

C.of E. Chaplain..............Captain W. Brown.

Vol 5

17/51

Confidential

War Diary

of

2/4th South Lancashire Regt

from June 1st 1917 to June 30th 1917

Robson Barclay
Major
2/4 South L.

Sheet VI
Army Form C. 2118.

WAR DIARY
or
INTELLIGENCE SUMMARY.
(Erase heading not required.)

Instructions regarding War Diaries and Intelligence
Summaries are contained in F.S. Regs., Part II.
and the Staff Manual respectively. Title pages
will be prepared in manuscript.

Hour, Date, Place			Summary of Events and Information	Remarks and references to Appendices
JUNE 1ST 1917		RUE MARLE Area	2nd Lieut A.E.WATSON evacuated to Hospital May 31st	RJG
	10.15 pm	"	Relieves the 2/5th S.Lan R in the RUE du BOIS Subsection	RJG
2nd 3rd 4th		RUE du BOIS Subsection	BOIS GRENIER Sector Relief completed 10.15 pm	RJG
		RUE du BOIS Subsection	2nd Lieuts A.H.LAYHE, J.H.LEACH, W.L.THOMPSON, Epsilon	RJG
5th		"	Joined from 4th Res Bn S.Lan.R.	RJG
			Right Coy occupied new Coy HdQrs. BARA was shelled by enemy	RJG
6th		"	2nd Lieut E.L.ROBINSON returned to duty from 4th Res Bn S.Lan R	RJG
7th		"	2nd Lieut T.D.FITZGERALD reported for duty from 4th Res Bn S.Lan R	RJG
8th		"	2nd Lieut J.TAYLOR reported for duty from 4th Res Bn S.Lan R	RJG
			Silent Raid on a dam German House failed unsuccessful	RJG
9th	10.55 pm	"	2nd Lieut A.I.JACKSON evacuated to Hospital	RJG
		RUE MARLE AREA	Relieved by 2/5th S.Lan R Relief completed 10.55 pm. Proceeded to billets	RJG
			Patrol under 2nd Lieut Q.B.SMITH & D.J.MEARNS met 3 OR enemies	RJG Appendix of
			enemy trenches inflicting two casualties	
			Patrol under 2nd Lieut J.H.LEACH and 4 OR bombed enemy	RJG
			occ slightly wounded concentration G. ADS	
			Casualties during tour 5 Wounded (Fierce clases) and available	RJG
10th		RUE MARLE Area	B.Hd Qrs Shelled 10th 4.25-5.9's	RJG
11th	12.0 pm 8.30 am	"	Bn Hd Qrs Shelled 12 am & 6.30 pm	RJG
12th		"	Bn Hd Qrs Shelled 1.30 am Lieut and Adj S.JERSON to ADS	RJG
13.9/14	1.30 am	RUE.MARLE AREA		RJG
15th		"	2nd Lieut D.W.WINSTANLEY evacuated ADS	RJG

Sheet VII
Army Form C. 2118.

WAR DIARY
or
INTELLIGENCE SUMMARY.
(Erase heading not required.)

Hour, Date, Place	Summary of Events and Information	Remarks and references to Appendices
JUNE 15th/17 10.30 p.m. RUE DU BOIS SubSector BOISGRENIER Sector	Silent Raid on enemy trenches by Officers and 120 OR Chinered into two parties	Ref Trench Map 36 NW 1/10,000 RJC
	Right Raid under Capt R.A.FOX Left Raid under Capt J. GLASCOTT Copy of Operation order NO 13 attached Copy of Report on Raid attached Raid unsuccessful Casualties 1 Killed 4 Slightly wounded	Appendix H I RJC
16th	RUE MARLE Area	
17th 11.30 a.m.	Relieved the 2/5th S.Lan R RUE DU BOIS SubSector Relief complete 11.30 a.m	RJC
18	RUE DU BOIS SubSector	RJC
19	" Rev Cypn W BROWN OofE evacuated to Hospital Sick	RJC
20	" Lt Col T.H.S. MARCHANT won 1st Army ¼ hp Motor Officers Chargers at XI Corps Horse Show	RJC
21-22	RUE DU BOIS SubSector "	RJC
23rd	" 2nd Lieut J. BROOKES to relieve to duty from Hospital	RJC
	" Lieut F.H. DICKETTS to return to duty from 4th Res Bn S.Lan R	RJC
	" Lieut and Acty G. JEPSON to return from Hospital	RJC
	" 2nd Lieut D.W.WINSTANLEY reported from ADS	RJC
24th	"	
25th 11 p.m.	Relieved by 2/5th S Lan R Relief complete 11 p.m concentrated to BMG RUE MARLE Area	RJC
	RUE MARLE Area Enemy guns during our relief with the exception of Minnies	RJC
26th	" Casualties during tour 3 wounded 4 wounded & slightly wounded	RJC
27th	" 2nd Lieut T. MOINEUX to return to duty from 4th Res Bn S.Lan R	RJC
28	"	RJC
29	" Area Shelled & Church an YMCA hit	RJC
30	" Area Cora Poaci shelled at 10.30 pm	RJC
	" Area and Huach Shelter 3 Q m	RJC
	Casualties Officers 1 wounded (instructor on a duty) OR 3 killed 28 wounded HO attached 12 officers TMB	RJC RJC
	TOTAL STRENGTH on June 30th Officers 43 Instructor 2 officers TMB OR 822 12 OR 7 MB	

Robson J. Chorley
Lieut
2/4 S.Lan R

FOLLOWING MESSAGE RECEIVED.-   Appendix G

172nd Infantry Brigade.

      G.96/96, 10.6.17.AAA   G.O.C. Division congratulates 2/Lieut: G.B. Smith 2/Lieut D.J. Mearns and three other ranks of PAIR on the initiative and dash shown when on patrol work in the German lines on the night of 9th/10th June AAA He hopes to have an opportunity soon of congratulating them personally on their excellent work

                                57th Division.

     II.

                                                 B.M.478. 10/6/17.

O.C. 2/4th Bn South Lancashire Rgt.

      The G.O.C. is very pleased to be able to forward this report.

10/6/17.   Sgd........T. Lucy, Captain,
                                                  Brigade Major,
                                       172nd Infantry Brigade.

Appendix H

OPERATION ORDER No.13   COPY No. 9.
by
Lt. Col. T.H.S. Marchant,
commanding
2/4th Bn South Lancashire Regiment.   15/6/17.

Ref: Trench Map 36 N.W. $\frac{1}{10,000}$
and aeroplane photographs of
RUE du BOIS Sub-sector.

INFORMATION. I. Silent Raiding Parties furnished by the 2/4th Bn South Lancashire Rgt., comprising 9 Officers and 100 Other Ranks, will raid the enemy trenches on the night of the 15th/16th June.
The enemy wire is being cut at places according to the attached programme, and patrols with the assistance of Vickers Guns are working to keep all the gaps open, although it is not intended that entry should be made at all the gaps.

INTENTION. II. The object of these raids is :-
    (1) To harass the enemy along his front.
    (2) To kill or capture as many of the enemy as possible, by attacking his posts and bombing his dug-outs.
    (3) To obtain identification.

GENERAL PLAN
OF ACTION. III. The Raiding Parties are divided into two main portions - the Right and Left Raids; the former operating on the Right and the latter operating on the Left of the RUE du BOIS Salient.
Each raid will consist of two or more assaulting parties and a covering party.
Parties will leave our trenches at Zero Hour and cross N.M.L. in single file, but before entry will form on their leader and force an entry closing with the enemy without hesitation should he open with bombs or fire.
Lewis Gunners will advance with Magazines in position and be prepared to open fire from the hip or from the ground without a moment's delay, in the event of the enemy suddenly opening from the gap or parapet at close range with rifle or automatic rifle fire.
For this reason the parties which include Lewis Guns should advance with the guns well forward.
Parties on entering the enemy trenches will attack him with determination; trenches will be searched and dug-outs bombed.
Parties will remain in the enemy trenches for at least 20 minutes before withdrawing, their duty being to find him and do him damage.
Should no enemy be encountered within the limits laid down for their action in these orders, leaders of parties will extend their search.
Bombs are not to be used except for dug-outs or to cover the withdrawal: The bayonet and the Lewis Gun must be regarded as the chief weapon of offence.

DISTRIBUTION IV. The RIGHT Raid will be composed as follows :-

    O.C. Raid   - Captain Fox.

    Mearn's Party. - 2nd Lt. Mearns.
                        1 Lewis Gun,
                        20 Other Ranks.

    Robinson's Party. 2nd Lt. Robinson.
                        1 Lewis Gun.
                        20 Other Ranks.

Rhodes' Party. (Covering Party)
         2nd Lt. Rhodes.
         10 Other Ranks.

TOTAL - 4 Officers. 50 Other Ranks. 2 Lewis Guns.

The LEFT Raid will be composed as follows:-

O.C. Raid -   Captain Glascott.

Smith's Party. - 2nd Lt. Smith.
         8 Other Ranks.

Fairclough's Party.
         Lieut Fairclough.
         16 Other Ranks.

Harding's Party. Sgt Harding.
         8 Other Ranks.

Taylor's Party. (Covering Party).
         2nd Lt. Taylor.
         1 Lewis Gun.
         10 Other Ranks.

TOTAL - 4 Officers, 42 Other Ranks, 1 Lewis Gun.

In addition to the above, each O.C. Raid will have with himin our front line, 8 Stretcher Bearers, 4 Runners, and 2 Telephonists with their instruments.
For detail of each party see Appendix 'B'

ORDERS FOR RAIDING PARTIES.

V. RIGHT Raid.

Captain Fox will conduct operations from I.21.c.50.80. where he will be in communication with Advanced Battalion Headquarters by telephone, and with his Raiding Parties by Runners.

Mearn's Party. - will leave our trenches at I.21.c.50.80. and will follow the Railway and enter at I.21.c.72.30., blocking the right with Bombers and covering the C.T. with a Lewis Gun.
If the Lewis Gun can be well placed on the enemy parapet or parados, it should cause casualties to any of the enemy attempting to reach the Front Line by the C.T. or overland.
The Assaulting Parties will proceed left handed along his front and supervision trenches for a distance of 40 yards, clearing dug-outs as they go.
This party will withdraw by the place of entry.

Robinson's Party. - will leave our trenches at I.21.c.70.80. and enter at I.21.c.85.53., blocking the left with bombers and covering the C.T. with a Lewis Gun.
The Assaulting Parties will move to the right - otherwise the whole will act similarly to Mearn's Party.

Rhodes' Party. - will follow Robinson's Party, and will cover the operations from a point in N.M.L. at I.21.c.70.60. paying particular attention to the left flank.
In the event of an enemy attack on the flanks in N.M.L. this party will lie close until he has approached, when it will go in with the bayonet.
This party will cover the withdrawal of the other parties before coming in.

LEFT Raid.

O.C. Raid.- Captain Glascott will conduct the operations. from I.15.d.40.10., where he will be in communication with Battalion Headquarters and with his Raiding Parties by telephone and Runners.

Smith's Party. - will leave our trenches at I.15.d.45.10.
and will move by a route already reconnoitred and enter
at I.21.b.78.40., leaving two men on the parapet, attacking the Sentry post located near the point of entry.
Should this post fail to be in the position expected, the
party will proceed left handed along the front trench towards the head of the C.T. at I.21.b.90.28, leaving two
men to hold the front trench on the right of the point of
entry.
This party will withdraw by the place of entry.
Before withdrawing a "Booby trap" of bombs and trip line
will be placed at a suitable place to catch the enemy
should he follow up.

Fairclough's Party. - will leave our trenches at I.15.d.50.
20., and will move by a route already reconnoitred and
enter at I.22.a.18.45.
Parties consisting of 1 N.C.O. and 4 men will immediately
proceed to the right and left for ten yards to secure the
flanks, while the remainder push down the C.T. opposite
the point of entry, bombing the dug-outs as they go.
Before withdrawing, this party will set a "Booby Trap" near
the head of the C.T.
This party will withdraw by the place of entry.

Harding's Party. - will leave our trenches at I.16.c.10.60.
and will move by a route already reconnoitred and enter at
I.22.a.45.70. leaving two men on the parapet at the point
of entry.
This party which has been detailed to cover the left flank
of the Raid and to cause a diversion, will, after entering
the enemy trenches, act according to circumstances, not
losing sight of the fact that any opportunity for damaging
the enemy must be taken.
Should the wind be favourable for taking a smoke barrage
northwards, this party will carry forward 4 Smoke Candles
which will be lit in the enemy trenches with the purpose
of attracting his attention towards the north and away from
the main operations.
If the wind does not favour this action no smoke candles
will be taken.
This party will withdraw by the place of entry after setting
"Booby Traps" according to circumstances.

Taylor's Party. - (Covering Party). - will follow Fairclough's Party after an interval of five minutes, and will
proceed to I.21.b.90.70 in N.M.L., where it will extend to
the right and remain watching the flanks and covering the
Assaulting Parties until the whole have withdrawn and an
order is received from O.C. Left Raid to come in.
A telephone instrument will accompany this party.

EQUIPMENT. VI. All ranks taking part will black their faces and remove
all identification marks such as identity discs, badges
and numerals, and yellow arm badges. A label with name,
number, and religion inscribed thereon will be attached
to the third button of the jacket.
Articles with which parties are equipped are shown in
Appendix A.

DISTINGUISHING
MARKS.   VII. The labels mentioned in the previous order act in this
capacity.

SIGNALS.   VIII. S.O.S. signals will be suspended during the Raid.
The signal for the withdrawal of parties will be blasts
on the whistle given by their leader.
The Signal for a general withdrawal will be a succession
of White Parachute Lights sent up from Advanced Battalion
Headquarters.

COMMUNICATION.	IX.	Telephone communication will be established between Advanced Battalion Headquarters and Headquarters of the Officers Commanding Right and Left Raids by 6.0.pm, on the 15th inst., and communication opened by 9.0.pm. For Code Words see Appendix C.
MEDICAL.	X.	The Medical Officer will arrange for Advanced Regimental Aid Posts, one at Advanced Battalion Headquarters and one at I.15.d.30.05. - these will be opened by 9.0.pm. on the 15th inst. Wounded will be evacuated from these posts by WELLINGTON AVENUE and WINE AVENUE respectively.
ARTILLERY.	XI.	Arrangements have been made for the guns covering the RUE du BOIS Sub-sector to fire on certain points in rear of the enemy front line in case of emergency. The request for them to open will only be made through Advanced Battalion Headquarters.
ZERO HOUR.	XII.	Zero Hour will be at 10.30.pm. on the 15th inst.
REPORTS.	XIII.	Advanced Battalion Headquarters will be at I.21.a.40.45., in the Support Line between the RUE du BOIS C.T. and SALOP AVENUE. Constant communication will be maintained between O.C. Raids and Advanced Battalion Headquarters, and the Officer Commanding must be kept informed of all movements and events as they occur.

Copy No. 1. File.
    2. H.Q. 172nd Inf Bde.
    3. O.C. Right Raid.
    4. O.C. Left Raid.
    5. Battn Signalling Officer.
    6. O.C. Artillery Group.
    7. O.C. 2/5 S.L.R.
    8) - Spare Copies. WAR DIARY
    9)

(Sgd) T.H.S. Marchant,
    Lieut Colonel,
    Commanding
2/4th Bn South Lancashire Rgt.

Programme of action of Medium Trench Mortars
on the Brigade Sector up to the 15th inst.

10th inst. -   Target - Wire at I.22.a.45.65.

11th inst. -   Target - Wire between I.21.d.00.75. - 06.78.

12th inst. -   Target - Wire between I.22.a.12.40. - 20.47.

13th inst. -   Target - Wire at I.21.c.85.53.

14th inst. -   Target - Wire between I.16.d.20.38. - 25.45.

15th inst. -   Target - Wire at I.22.a.77.83.

Appendix I

REPORT ON SILENT RAID CARRIED OUT BY 2/4th BATTALION
SOUTH LANCASHIRE REGIMENT, ON THE NIGHT OF JUNE 15th
16th, 1917.

1. WIRE.

Previous to the Raid taking place, the wire was systematically cut at various points opposite RUE DU BOIS Sub-Sector every night from the 10th to the 15th inst. inclusive. The gaps so formed were kept under constant Machine Gun fire throughout the nights. The Machine Gun fire apparently prevented the enemy re-wiring his gaps but did not succeed in preventing him throwing over large knife rests, which formed serious obstacles and in two cases prevented our Raiding Parties from entering.

2. OPERATION ORDERS.

A copy of the artillery orders for covering the Raiding Parties is attached herewith.
A copy of the Orders for the Raid by O.C. 2/4th Bn South Lancashire Regt. has already been forwarded to you.

3. REPORT ON ACTION.

Two parties gained an entrance into the enemy's trenches, 1 party of the Right Raid (Captain Fox) and 1 Party of the Left Raid (Captain Glascott).
The enemy showed signs of great alertness throughout the night and appeared to be expecting us. A searchlight was used, and at midnight a considerable number of small gas shells, which have been fired before on this Sub-Sector, were put over, hampering the latter part of the operations very considerably.
On the left flank of our Left Raid the enemy employed a strong fighting patrol, which was encountered and held off by the left party.

RIGHT RAID. Captain Fox.

Mearn's Party. Left our lines at 11.15.pm. and when half way across came under rifle and automatic rifle fire. They continued to the enemy wire where they found that the gap had been filled with "knife-rests" with strong barbed concertina wire on top. The Knife-rests could not be moved although attempts were made continuously to force an entry. Some pineapples and bombs were sent at this party, and at midnight a searchlight was turned on and machine gun fire opened. Lieut. Mearns tried several other places without success, and continued his efforts until 2.0.am. when he withdrew, experiencing some discomfort from gas-shells which were just over at that hour.

Robinson's Party. Left our lines at 11.20.pm. and entered the enemy trenches without difficulty. On moving to the right according to orders the trench was found to be wired up inside. When Lieut Robinson began to move his men back to the parapet with the intention of going along it and entering again if possible beyond the wire in gaps, the enemy opened from his Support Line with very heavy rifle grenade barrage, causing casualties - one killed and three wounded. This barrage was extremely heavy. Lieut Robinson remained with his runner on the parapet for a considerable time while his party withdrew. The enemy was content to fire rifle grenades and machine guns from his Support Line with the assistance of a searchlight, but did not make an attempt to man his front line at this point. The body of the killed man was brought back to our lines.

LEFT RAID. (Captain Glascott). Parties left at 11.0.pm.

Smith's Party. Lost direction and failed to find place of entry. This party returned at 3.0.am. This party was obliged to use Gas Helmets after 2.0.am. on account of Gas Shells.

Fairclough's Party. Found the gap allotted to it filled up with "knife-rests" near the enemy parapet, and could see the parapet was manned by a few men. He made three attempts to get through the wire, first with all his party and afterwards twice with a few men only. Pineapples and Grenades were fired at this party - one man was slightly wounded. The party returned at 2.25.am.

Harding's Party. Entered the enemy trenches at I.20.a.45.70. without opposition of any sort. Sergeant Harding reports that he found the trenches here entirely unheld and that there appeared to be a gap in the line. He searched to the right and left for 50 yards each way, and was then recalled by the men he left on the parapet, who reported a strong enemy patrol working behind them from the N. This party had been in the trenches for about ½ an hour when the patrol was reported and had found nothing. The N.C.O. took his party of 7 men towards the enemy patrol, which appeared to be about 30 strong and as if attempting to cut off Fairclough's Party. The enemy divided and withdrew on his approach, throwing bombs. Sergeant Harding inflicted several casualties to these parties with bombs and rifle fire. Lieut Fairclough and his officers confirm Sergeant Harding's statements. The party returned at 2.25.am. without loss.

4. CASUALTIES. Our total casualties were one killed and four wounded.

5. IDENTIFICATIONS. No identifications were obtained.

APPENDIX B.

DETAIL OF PARTIES.

	L.Gunners.	Bombers.	N.C.Os.	Riflmn.	Runners.	Telephonists	Str Brs.	Party Total.	Raid Totals
RIGHT RAID.									
H.Q.					4	2	8	14	
Mearns Party	2	4	3	10	1	-	-	20.	
Robinsons "	2	4	3	10	1	-	-	20	
Rhodes "	-	-	-	9	1	1	1	10	64
LEFT RAID.									
H.Q.					4	2	8	14	
Smiths Party			1	6	1	-	-	8	
Fairclough's Party.		4	3	8	1	-	-	16	
Hardings Pty.	-	-	1	7	-	-	-	8	
Taylors Pty.	2	-	1	5	-	2	1	10	56
	6.	12.	12.	55.	13.	6.	16.		120.

WAR DIARY or INTELLIGENCE SUMMARY

Army Form C. 2118.
Sheet VIII

HEADQUARTERS 2nd R.B 38
Date 1.8.17

ORDERLY ROOM
S.O. 2/306
1 AUG 1917
2/4 Q. R. France Vol 1

Instructions regarding War Diaries and Intelligence Summaries are contained in F.S. Regs., Part II and the Staff Manual respectively. Title pages will be prepared in manuscript.

72ND 2.0?pm INFANTRY BRIGADE

Hour, Date, Place	Summary of Events and Information	Remarks and references to Appendices
JULY 1st 4.0pm RUE MARLE Area	Rest Billets	RJC
2nd "	"	RJC
3rd "	"	RJC
4th "	"	RJC
5th "	"	RJC
1.10am 6th "	Draft of 3 Other Ranks joined for duty	RJC
9.00am 7th "	2nd Lieut A.H. LAYHE evacuated to Hospital	RJC
1.35am 8th "	Railway Shelters Enemy aeroplane Spotting By Posns	RJC
9th "	ARMENTIERES Ry circa By positions Sheller Capt W.E. SMITH & 2/Lt joined for duty	RJC
10th RUE du BOIS Subsector	2nd Lieut J.H. HUGHES 4th Res Bn S Lan R joined for duty. Sniper. Enemy Bns for usminner	RJC
11th "	Relieved 4/5th Bn S Lan R RUE du BOIS Subsector BOIS GRENIER Sector. Trenches and OPs on bad state of repair Hostile Enemy alttm'tre raid night of 6/7th	RJC
12th "	Relief complete 10-50am	RJC
13th "	Quiet day 3 Heavy Minnie airburst over Subsectors own Artillery fairly active	RPC
14th "	Quiet day	RPC
15th "	Associate active during day	RJC
1.30am 16th	Enemy TM's active during day	RJC
10.30am 17th	Enemy Artillery v TM's Active during day Our artillery v TM's active during day	RJC
2.30am 18th	Enemy fired about 150 T.Ms on our front line Own artillery active during day also Enemy TM's 4 Gas shells put over Subsidiary Line Quiet day except for retaliation to own M.T.M's 2nd Lieut EL ROBINSON wounded evacuated to Hospital	RJC
	Enemy fired large number of T.M Gas shells between Willow Support and 2nd Support's otherwise Quiet 2nd Lieut C.A. LONGSHAW 4th Res Bn S Lan R wounded evacuated to Hospital Relieved by 6th 2/10 L/pool Regt (Scottish) relief complete 10-40 am and proceeded to Rest Billets RUE MARLE Area	RJC
19th Rest Billets RUE MARLE AREA	Casualties during tour of trenches 2 Officers wounded 9 O.R Wounded 2 Casualty Own Side: 1 O.R. wounded 5/7/17 2 O.R. wounded 7-7-17 on working party 1 O.R attacks 4 P.M. 4-7-17 artillery 1 O.R. wounded 17/7/17 on duty	RJC
20 "	2 D.R. wounded attached 505 Trenches Coy Quiet day	RJC
9.30am 21st H.E.1.30am	Brig-Genl G.A. LONGSMAN M.4 Res Bn S Lan R sick & wounded on O25. Dud 42 Enemy Naval Aeroplane dropped 3 bombs in place W RUE MARLE church ARMENTIERES Shelled Very large morning Gas Shells Scheme Bn HQrs RUE MARLE & ARMENTIERES	RJC
31st "	Quiet morning ARMENTIERES heavily shelled 2.0pm	RJC

Sheet IX
Army Form C. 2118.

WAR DIARY
INTELLIGENCE SUMMARY
(Erase heading not required.)

Instructions regarding War Diaries and Intelligence Summaries are contained in F.S. Regs., Part II. and the Staff Manual respectively. Title pages will be prepared in manuscript.

Hour, Date, Place		Summary of Events and Information	Remarks and references to Appendices
1917			
9.0 P.M. July 21st	RUE MARLE AREA	ARMENTIERES Bty heavily shelled from Station to Same Bay Barn also Bty Positions. Tout 100 hours also during night	RJC
9.0 A.M. 22nd	" "	Bty Positions shelled at morning. Enemy aeroplanes active shelling two enemy guns	RJC
2.30 P.M. 22nd – 6.10 P.M.	" "	CROWN PRINCE HOUSE heavily shelled with 5.9" & 8" shells. Partially demolished. Casualties Major R.J. Choly, 2/Lt E.W. Hodson wounded removed to Hospital; Capt W. Wilkins & Pte C. Clarkson wounded remained at duty. 3 O.R. wounded & evacuated to Hospital. 2 O.R. remained at duty.	O.R.U. B.
11.30 P.M. 22nd	" "	RUE MARLE and ARMENTIERES again shelled. Billets evacuated	O.R.U. B.
9 A.M. 23rd	" "	RUE MARLE evacuated. Bn H'quarters & rear billets established at ERQUINGHAM.	O.R.U. B.
10.30 P.M. 23rd	ERQUINGHAM	'C' Coy (58 Coy in line) heavily shelled with tear fumes gas shells	O.R.U. B.
10 A.M. 24th	"	51 casualties in 'C' Coy evacuated. 12 hours before any symptoms developed.	O.R.U. B.
– 8 P.M. 25th	"	Completion of salvage of CROWN PRINCE HOUSE. Practically all stores & equipment recovered.	O.R.U. B.
9.30 P.M. 26th	RUE de BOIS Subsector	Relieve No 9 Post R in RUE de BOIS Subsector. Relief completed by 11.45 P.M. 'D' Coy to Sam R in rest at ERQUINGHAM. Completing/ relieving. 'C' Coy No 9 Post R remain as 4 Coy. Special training.	O.R.U. B.
10.30 P.M. 27/28 – 4 A.M.	"	Subsid'd line heavily shelled with H.E. & Gas shells. Limber hit. 2 transport section killed. 1 O.R. wounded. 2 mules killed. Enemy act. very active during day, especially 77mm too of which focus fired on CONGATE "Minnie" abnormally quiet.	O.R.U. B.

APPENDIX.

Nominal Roll of Officers.

Lt. Col. T.H.S. Marchant.   17th Hussars.
Captain W. McClure
Lt & Adjutant, S. Jopson.   1st N.Stffs.
Lieut T. Thwaites.   2/5th E.N.Lancs Rgt. T.F
2nd Lt A.J. Watson.   4th East Lancs. T.F
Captain J. Glascott.   4th N. Staffs. SR
Captain R.A. Fox.
Captain H.A. Sawyer.
Captain V.C.D. Mills.

Lieut R.B. Fairclough.
Lieut R.P. Carter.
Lieut S.T. Quint.
Lieut C.G. Linnell.

2nd Lt. K.L. Gordon.
2nd Lt. J. Brookes.
2nd Lt. C.E. Clarkson.
2nd Lt. F.I. Jackson.
2nd Lt. G.B. Smith.   Northum Div: Cyclist Coy.
2nd Lt. A. Thompson.   7th W. Yorks. T.F.
2nd Lt. B. Milburn.   "
2nd Lt. H.L. Stevens.   5th Lpool Rgt.
2nd Lt. H.G. Rhodes.   7th Lpool Rgt.
2nd Lt. C.J. Grierson.   5th Lpool Rgt.
2nd Lt. E.J. Kearns.   5th Lpool Rgt.
2nd Lt. A.H. Grant.   3rd E.Lan R. S.R.
2nd Lt. F. Clegg.
2nd Lt. P.O. Platts.   P.O.
2nd Lt. A. Ritchie.
2nd Lt. D.W. Winstanley.
2nd Lt. W.L. Thompson.
2nd Lt. J.T. Fitzgerald.
2nd Lt. J. Taylor.
2nd Lt. E.H. Dicketts.
2nd Lt. T. Molyneux.
2nd Lt. J.M. Hughes.

Captain W.S. Smith.   C of E Chaplain,
                                     attached.

Sheet X.

Army Form C. 2118.

WAR DIARY
or
INTELLIGENCE SUMMARY.
(Erase heading not required.)

Instructions regarding War Diaries and Intelligence Summaries are contained in F.S. Regs., Part II. and the Staff Manual respectively. Title pages will be prepared in manuscript.

Hour Date	~~Hour, Date,~~ Place	Summary of Events and Information	Remarks and references to Appendices
11.45am 29.7.17	Rue de Bois Intersection	1 → M.T.M. fired opposite CHARDS FM & WINE AV on enemy wire. Retaliation heavy. ARMENTIERES again heavily shelled.	Wire B
9 P.M	"	Heavy bombardment of ARMENTIERES & areas behind. Enemy used H.E. & 4000 gas shells.	Wire B
12.15am-2.15am 29.7.17	"		
9 am 30.7.17	"	Two more cases sent to hospital suffering from symptoms of bronchitis. They were admitted at 9am on 23.7.17.	Wire B
9 pm 3/9/17 7 pm	"	T.M. shot during the day in retaliation to enemy operation. He fired 25. Headquartiers in COMPARTE locality and front line trenches much damaged.	Wire G
7.30 pm	"	'D' Coy arrived in billeting lines ready for service on at 1.30 a.m. 1.8.17. 2/Lt. Dr. WINSTANLEY left for sick leave to England & reported to Med. Offr.	Wire C
—	31/7/17	Total strength of Bn. on 31.7.17. 36 Officers including C of E chaplain & 713 other ranks. List of Officers attached (Appen at E.)	Wire G Willcocks Lt. Colonel Comdg Lt. Colonel Commanding 1st Bn R.

Sheet VI

Army Form C. 2118.

2/4 S Lanc. Rgt
Vol 7

WAR DIARY
or
INTELLIGENCE SUMMARY.
(Erase heading not required.)

Instructions regarding War Diaries and Intelligence Summaries are contained in F.S. Regs., Part II. and the Staff Manual respectively. Title pages will be prepared in manuscript.

Hour, Date, Place	Summary of Events and Information	Remarks and references to Appendices
1.30 a.m. 8.17 RUE DE BOIS Sub-sector	"D" Coy under Captain D' successfully raided the enemy trenches at J.21.a.30.35 — 10.43 — 30.31 — 40.43. Many German rifles, 2 machine guns & much booty. Our casualties 4 wounded all (slightly) & 16 casualties from A to J.4ths. Enemy losses 3 officers & about equal [illegible] "D" Coy dug-out on [illegible] & tunnel [illegible] entrance now full in [illegible] [illegible]	Co. att. 6. [illegible]
2.8.17		[illegible]
1.30 P.M 4.8.17	Relieved by 7/10 R. of F. Rel[illegible] at Rue des Bois & ERQUINGHEM. Coy complete by 11.30 P.M. Total Casualties for tour of place 2 killed 2/ wounded (one of Coy) 2 wounded above. All other [illegible] & [illegible] to [illegible].	[illegible]
— 5.8.17		[illegible]
11 A.M 11.8.17 RUE DE ERQUINGHEM	At LEITH WALK billets 2 officers & [illegible] wounded [illegible] 2 Riflemen [illegible]	[illegible]
— 9.8.17	Ordinary training to H.M.G.S. [illegible] who were in [illegible] on [illegible] D.R.O. 4a.9.8.17	See Appendix K attached
10 P.M 12.8.17 RUE DE BOIS Sub-sector	Relieved 7/10 R. of F. in RUE DE BOIS Sub-sector. Relief complete by 11.5 P.M.	[illegible]
— 13.8.17	"D" Coy carried out attack R.T.M. for Question 1.8.17 a.p.m. L[illegible] Coy. D.R.O. 4a.13.8.17	See Appendix L attached
[illegible] 14.8.17	To all Bns. serves like usual. Trench Releases. [illegible]	[illegible]
Gale PM 14.8.17	To Leith Walk & Rue [illegible]	[illegible]
5.30 PM 16.8.17	R.A.F. Rd. s [illegible] & Sunday Croop. [illegible] [illegible] [illegible] grid line [illegible] [illegible] on cavalry. D.R.O. 4a.16.8.17	[illegible]
— 18.8.17	Relieved by 1/9 L.F. in Rue DE Bois Sub-sect. Relief	[illegible]
30.P.M 20.8.17	[illegible]	[illegible]

Sheet 12. Army Form C. 2118.

WAR DIARY
or
INTELLIGENCE SUMMARY.
(Erase heading not required.)

Hour, Date, Place	Summary of Events and Information	Remarks and references to Appendices
PLACE. Regt BILLETS ERQUINGHEM		
29/8/17		
10 P.M. 28-8-17 RUE DE BOIS Sub-sector	Returned to No 2 Bn R in RUE DE BOIS Sub-sector. Relief Complete by 10.35 PM	issue 40. issue 40
4.30 P.M. 31.8.17 "	Entraining instruction school to giving to sub-sector for 1 Army Q "H" M" F". Tn B"s: 4, 5th Ave & 18 Div. Bn Lewis obtained. Retaliation light.	issue 46.
31.8.17 "	Total strength of Bn as 31.8.17. 35. Officers and 681. Other ranks. Nominal Roll of Officers attached.	Roll of Officers of Bn of 31.8.17 Appendix "N" issue 40.

William W. Holmes, Major
for Lt. Colonel
Comdg 2nd Bn R.

Appendix "K".

Extract from 57th Divisional Routine Orders,
dated 9th August, 1917.

1214. **MILITARY MEDAL.**

Under authority delegated by the Field Marshal Commanding-in-Chief, the Corps Commander has awarded the MILITARY MEDAL to the undernamed N.C.O's and Men for gallantry and devotion to duty in action :-
(Athy:- XI Corps Routine Orders No.1911(2) dated 8/8/17).
(Date of Award 4/8/17).

No.201208. Sgt Harry KIRK, "M" Battalion S.Lancs Regt.
On the night of July 31st - August 1st during a successful raid on the enemy's trenches opposite the..........salient, South of........... this N.C.O. led his party into the enemy's trenches in spite of severe opposition from the enemy lying in No Man's Land. The Germans were dispersed and the trenches entered. Several Germans were bayoneted and a prisoner brought back, thereby securing an identification. Sgt Krik's fearless conduct was a great example to his men.

201189, Pte Alexander LITTLE, "M" Battalion S.Lancs Regt.
For bravery on the night July 31st - August 1st, 1917, during a raid on the enemy's trenches opposite the.........salient, South of.............The party which Pte LITTLE was with, met with severe opposition. They fought their way into the enemy's trenches, where Pte LITTLE was attacked by a German. He overcame him after a struggle and made him prisoner, bringing him back to our own lines, thereby securing an identification.

No.201538. Sgt William WOODWARD, "M" Battalion S.Lancs Regt.
For good leadership during a successful raid on the enemy's trenches opposite the..........salient, South of.......... on the night July 31st - August 1st, 1917. A T.M.Bomb fell among the party commanded by this N.C.O., wounding several and disorganizing the party. Sgt WOODWARD rallied the men and led them into the enemy's trenches. The party was responsible for inflicting severe casualties on the Germans. On withdrawal, he carried a badly wounded man back to our trenches through the barrage.

No.202229, Sgt Thos.Henry GREGSON, "M" Battalion S.Lancs Regt.
For good leadership during a successful raid on the enemy's trenches, opposite the............salient, South of............ on the night of July 31st - August 1st, 1917. Considerable opposition was encountered in "No Man's Land" from a party of Germans who were waiting in front of their wire. Sgt GREGSON immediately charged the enemy with his party and succeeded in entering their trenches. In spite of being wounded he secured a prisoner and brought him in.

No.202236. Pte Arthur DANIELS, "M" Battalion S.Lancs Regt.
For fearless conduct on the night of July 31st -August 1st, 1917, during a raid on the enemy's trenches opposite the....... salient, South of.......... Pte DANIELS and 1 other man encountered 5 Germans outside the enemy wire. Two Germans were immediately shot, but the remaining three wounded the man with Pte DANIELS. Pte DANIELS then bayoneted one of them and put the other two to flight. He brought in the gas mask intact of the man he killed.

No.201286. Pte. James WARBURTON, "M" Battalion S.Lancs Regt.
For bravery on the night July 31st - August 1st, 1917, during a raid on the enemy's trenches opposite the......... South of........ The party he was in charge of met with severe opposition in "No Man's Land". In spite of most of the party being wounded he pressed on with the remainder, and entered the enemy's trenches. He personally bayoneted a German.

Appendix "M"

Extract from 57th Divisional Routine Orders dated
18th August, 1917.

1290. **MILITARY CROSS.**

Under authority granted by His Majesty the King, the Field Marshal Commanding-in-Chief has awarded the MILITARY CROSS to the undernamed officer for gallantry and devotion to duty in action :-

(Date of Award 14/8/17.)
(Athy:- MS/H/6317 dated 14/8/17.

2nd Lieut. Alexander Henry GRANT, S.Lancs Regt,
attd "M" Bn. S.Lancs Regt.

For extremely good work on the night of July 31st/August 1st, during a raid on the enemy's trenches opposite ....salient, South of.............This officer was responsible for marking out the place of assembly and routes up to the enemy's wire with tapes. In coming to the point of Assembly in No Man's Land a column lost its way. 2nd Lieut GRANT went in search of it and guided the party into position just in time to prevent the raid failing. He personally did all the preliminary reconnaissance work for the operation. It was largely due to his work that the raid was a success. He did very good work after the raid taking out search parties for the wounded and missing.

Appendix "L"

Extract from 57th Divisional Routine Orders dated 13th August, 1917.

1252. <u>MILITARY CROSS.</u>
The Field Marshal Commanding-in-Chief has under authority granted by His Majesty the King, awarded the MILITARY CROSS to the undernamed for gallantry and devotion to duty in action :-
(Athy:- MS/H/6267 dated 9/8/17.)
(<u>Date of Award 9/8/17.</u>)

2nd Lieut. David James MEARNS, Liverpool Regt.,
attd "M" Battalion S. Lancs Regt.

For good leadership in a successful raid on the enemy's trenches opposite the...............salient, South of....... on the night of July 31st - August 1st. He led the raiding party into the German trenches in the face of severe opposition. He remained on the enemy parapet throughout the entire operation in spite of the enemy barraging his own trenches, showing an utter disregard for personal safety.
It was owing to his good handling of the men that the party was extricated with few casualties.

Appendix "N"

HEADQUARTERS.

```
Commanding Officer....................Lt.Col. T.H.S. Marchant.
Second in Command.....................Major W. McClure.
A/Adjutant............................Captain J. Thwaites.
Quarter Master........................2nd Lt. A.J. Watson.
Transport Officer.....................Lieut. R.P. Carter.
Intelligence Officer..................2nd Lt. A.H. Grant, M.C.,
Medical Officer.......................Captain W.C.D. Hills.
Signalling Officer....................2nd Lieut. C.E. Clarkson.
Lewis Gun Officer.                   }
Bombing Officer.......................} 2nd Lieut G.B. Smith.
Pioneer Officer.......................
C. of E. Chaplain..................... Rev. W.S. Smith.
```

A. Company.

Lieut R.B. Fairclough.
2nd Lt. J. Brookes.
2nd Lt. C.J. Grierson.
2nd Lt. J. Taylor.

B. Company.

Lieut. S.T. Quint.
2nd Lt. H.G. Rhodes.
2nd Lt. H.L. Stevens.
2nd Lt. F.I. Jackson.
2nd Lt. A. Ritchie.
2nd Lt. W.L. Thompson.

C. Company.

Captain C.G. Linnell.
2nd Lt. F. Clegg.
2nd Lt. J.D. Fitzgerald.
2nd Lt. T. Molyneux.
2nd Lt. J.M. Hughes.
2nd Lt. J.F. Tew.

D. Company.

Captain R.A. Fox.
Captain B. Milburn.
2nd Lt. K.L. Gordon.
2nd Lt. D.J. Mearns, M.C.,

```
Brigade Bombing Officer...............Lieut. H.S. Sawyer.
Pioneer Company.......................2nd Lt. P.O. Platts.
Attached 57th Division................Captain J. Glascott.
Attached XI Corps.....................Lieut. S. Jepson.
O.C. Brigade School...................Captain A. Thompson.
Base on Medical Grounds...............Lieut. E.H. Dicketts.
```

35807. W16879/M1879 500,000 3/17 R.T. (1074) Forms W3091/3   Army Form W.3091.

Cover for Documents.

Nature of Enclosures.

War Diary

3/4 S Lancs Regt

Notes, or Letters written.

WAR DIARY
or
INTELLIGENCE SUMMARY.
(Erase heading not required.)

Army Form C. 2118.

Sheet 13.

ORDERLY ROOM
1 OCT 1917

Instructions regarding War Diaries and Intelligence Summaries are contained in F.S. Regs., Part II. and the Staff Manual respectively. Title pages will be prepared in manuscript.

Hour, Date, Place	Summary of Events and Information	Remarks and references to Appendices
8 pm 1.9.17 Rue de Bois Sect.	Relief of "QUEENS" & "YORKS" from Front with 4.25th & 6th Rifle Brig.	App. 6
8:15 Pm 2.9.17 "	[illegible] C.R. Command. Major of Bde arrived from Base	App. 6
10 am 4.9.17 "	Orchard Reserve relieved by Bramm. 2 O.R's wounded. Relief during 10 minute bombardment. 2 O.R gassed.	App. 6
10. P.m 5.9.17 "	Relieved by the 10th Bn. K. Royal R: Relief Coy 4.5 by 10.30 P.m. Tour casualties for tour. Officers: Nil. O.R. 1 killed 7 wounded	App. 6
— 7.9.17 Rest Billets Erquinghem.	2/Lt T Rayland & Lt A.M. Lampin arrived from England & joined Battn.	App. 6
— 9.9.17 "	Lt. Col. J.H.L Guernaud assumed temporary command of 11th Bn. Royal Regt. Major W. M Oliver command & blew.	App. 6
11.am 11.9.17 "	Erquinghem shelled by hostile 5.9 howitzers, during walk. 20 fell in about 30 minutes. No damage & no casualties.	App. 6
10 pm 13.9.17 Rue de Bois and Section	Relieved the 2/6 Lord Regt in Rue de Bois Sec. with Relief Coy 6. to 10 pm.	App. 6
3.30 P.m 14.9.17 "	Lille Post O.P. blown in. Skylarker to N.T.M.G. Mi. Are killed. 16 wounded & Artillery fire Reading Line killed 2 m & wounded 5 at O.R.	App. 6
2.30 pm 15.9.17 "	Enemy fired gas shells on our line from 10.2 pm. Usual weather position	App. 6
6. pm 17.9.17 "	Relieved by 11th Bn Royal Scots Fusiliers; Relief complete by 11.30 p.m. Casualties for Tour 11 O.R wounded.	App. 6
D'une — "	One Platoon & Lewis Gun per Coy is in resent Bn. O.P. from B.S.and 4 platoons & reserve lines by Pier 30 Inorder to combat the new enemy Houses. Roy Hollered into Rest Billets at Le Nouvean Monde. Road lights thereunder of 393 Rue du Bois into Army Reserve.	App. 6

WAR DIARY
or
INTELLIGENCE SUMMARY

Army Form C. 2118

Sheet 14

Place	Date	Hour	Summary of Events and Information	Remarks and references to Appendices
BELLERIVE	19/9/17	—	Moved by route march into billets at BELLERIVE via ESTAIRES & HINGES (12 miles).	(over)
PALFART & LIVOSSART (Training Area)	24/9/17	—	Moved from BELLERIVE via LILLERS & WESTERHAM to training area. Billets in PALFART & LIVOSSART (9 miles). No operation orders issued in whole Batt.	(over)
"	24/9/17	10 P.m.	Lt. Col. Mitchell assumed command of Battn.	(over)
"	24/9/17	—	Strength of 12 O.R. around from base.	(over)
"	3/9/17	—	Strength of 6 Ru. 37 Officers & 894 O.R. Nominal roll of Officers attached. (Appendix O.)	(over) Appendix O.

W. Downing. Major
7c Bn. Rifle Brigade

2/4th Bn South Lancashire Rgt.   Appendix "O"

HEADQUARTERS.

```
Commanding Officer...................Lt.Colonel T.H.S. Marchant.
Second in Command....................Major W. McClure.
A/Adjutant...........................Captain J. Thwaites.
Quarter Master.......................Lieut. P.A. McWilliam.
Transport Officer....................Lieut. R.P. Carter.
Intelligence Officer.................2nd Lt. A.H. Grant.M.C.,
Medical Officer......................Captain W.C.D. Hills.
Signalling Officer...................2nd Lt. C.E. Clarkson.
Lewis Gun Officer )
Bombing Officer    )................2nd Lt. G.B. Smith.
Pioneer Officer......................
C. of E. Chaplain....................Rev. W.S. Smith.
```

"A" Company.

Captain B. Milburn.
Lieut. R.B. Fairclough.
2nd Lt. C.G. Grierson.
2nd Lt. J. Taylor.
2nd Lt. A.J. Watson.

"B" Company.

Captain A. Thompson.
2nd Lt. H.G. Rhodes.
2nd Lt. F.I. Jackson.
2nd Lt. H.L. Stevens.
2nd Lt. A. Ritchie.

"C" Company.

Captain C.G. Linnell.
2nd Lt. F. Clegg.   (Course)
2nd Lt. J.D. Fitzgerald.   (Course)
2nd Lt. T. Molyneux.
2nd Lt. J.M. Hughes.   (Hospital)
2nd Lt. J.F. Tew.
2nd Lt. J. Brookes.

"D" Company.

Captain R.A. Fox.
Lieut. S.T. Quint.
2nd Lt. K.L. Gordon.
2nd Lt. D.J. Mearns.M.C.,
2nd Lt. W.L. Thompson.
2nd Lt. T.D. Layland.   (Course)
2nd Lt. A.M. Temple.   "

```
Brigade Bombing Officer..............Lieut H.S. Sawyer.
Attached 57th Division...............Captain J. Glascott.
    "    XI Corps....................Captain S. Jepson.
```

WAR DIARY or INTELLIGENCE SUMMARY

Army Form C. 2118.

(Erase heading not required.)

October 1917.

Instructions regarding War Diaries and Intelligence Summaries are contained in F.S. Regs., Part II. and the Staff Manual respectively. Title Pages will be prepared in manuscript.

Place	Date	Hour	Summary of Events and Information	Remarks and references to Appendices
EYRO SSART	4	—	Lt. Col. J.N. Marshant took over temporary command of 57th Inf. Bgde. from Lt. Col. W. Wilkie took over temporary command of the Bn.	Issue
"	6	10.11.4-5 pm	The Bn. & the remainder of 57th Bgde were inspected by the C.in.C. Field Marshal Sir Douglas Haig, at RELY near ST. HILAIRE.	Issue
"	17	—	57th Division transferred from IId Corps (1st Army) & VIII Corps (5th Army)	Issue
"	18	—	172nd Inf. Bgde moved by route march to CAMPAGNE near ST OMER. (Via LAIRES, FLECHIN) ESTRÉE-BLANCHE, MAMETZ.)	Issue
CAMPAGNE	19	—	172nd Inf. Bgde moved by motor bus to PROVEN, AREA No. 3. (Via EBBLINGHEM, ST. SYLVESTRE, CAPPEL, STEENVOORDE, WATOU.)	Issue
PROVEN	23	—	Moved to PROVEN, AREA No. 1	Issue
"	24	—	57th Division took over portion of front line of 34th Division. (Map Ref. Sheet 28 - BOUÉ) V.7. B. 71. 33. — V. 14. 6. 82. 85. 170th Bgde in support: 172nd Bgde in reserve.	Issue
ELVERDINGHE	26	5.40 am	170 C Bgde attacked in Division and Front; one rather Canadian Division objectives from being reached. (58th & 60th Division attacked on Right & Left March respectively.)	Issue
"	24/27	During night	172nd Bgde came out of ELVERDINGHE as Bgde in reserve.	Issue
"	29	—	57th Division transferred IX 2 Corps (5th Army)	R.a.q.
"	31	9.30 pm	Bn. and 3 Lives from issued by Enemy. Old aeroplane. Casualties: 2. O.R. Killed: 19. O.R. wounded. (Included 3 as gas.)	Received copy of Order
"	31	—	Strength 2 Bn. 38. Officers (including Chaplain attached). 898 Other Ranks.	(Received by A.P.)

W.W. Wilkie Major
2/c. 8 Lanc. R.

1875 Wt. W 593/826 1,000,000 4/15 I.B.C. & A. A.D.S.S./Forms/C. 2118.

Appendix "P"

NOMINAL ROLL OF OFFICERS.

2/4th Bn South Lancashire Regiment.

HEADQUARTERS.

Commanding Officer.	Lt.Col. T.H.S. Marchant.
Second in Command.	Major W. McClure.
Act: Adjutant.	Captain J. Thwaites.
Assist: Adjutant	2nd Lt. D.J. Mearns, M.C.,
Quarter Master.	Lieut. P.A. McWilliam.
Transport Officer.	Lieut. R.P. Carter.
Signalling Officer	Lieut. C.E. Clarkson.
Lewis Gun Officer.	Lieut. G.B. Smith.
Medical Officer.	Captain W.C.D. Hills.
C.of E. Chaplain (attached)	Rev. W.S. Smith.
Intelligence Officer.	2nd Lt. F. Clegg.

"A" Company.

Captain B. Milburn.
Lieut. R.P. Fairclough.
2nd Lt. C.J. Grierson.
2nd Lt. J. Taylor.
Lieut. A.J. Watson.

"B" Company.

Captain A. Thompson.
Lieut. F.I. Jackson.
Lieut. H.G. Rhodes.
2nd Lt. H.L. Stevens.
2nd Lt. A. Ritchie.

"C" Company.

Captain C.G. Linnell.
Lieut. J. Brookes.
Lieut. J.M. Hughes.
2nd Lt. J.F. Tew.
2nd Lt. J.D. Fitzgerald.
2nd Lt. T. Molyneux.

"D" Company.

Captain R.A. Fox.
Lieut. S.T. Quint.
Lieut. A.M. Temple.
Lieut. T.D. Layland.
2nd Lt. W.L. Thompson.

Att: 57th Div. H.Q.	Captain J. Glascott.
Att: XI A Corps H.Q.	Captain S. Jepson.
Brigade Bombing Officer.	Lieut. H.S. Sawyer.
172nd Inf. Bde. Pioneer Coy.	Lieut. K.L. Gordon.
Att: 172nd Inf Bde H.Qrs.	Lieut. A.H. Grant, M.C.,
Att: 556 (Glamorgan) Field Coy, R.E.,	2nd Lt. P.C. Platts.

WAR DIARY or INTELLIGENCE SUMMARY

Army Form C. 2118.

2/4 Bn. S. Lancs Rgt.

Sheet. 16.

November, 1917.

Place	Date	Hour	Summary of Events and Information	Remarks and references to Appendices
ELVERDINGHE	2.11.17	3 P.M.	Bn less transport & details moved from huts at ELVERDINGHE to MARSOUIN Fm Camp at PILKEM area. Carrying parties of 450 each night moved to carry up to line & dumps to complete tracks & front line rations. Bn now Bgde Reserve. Casualties: 3.11.17. 2. O.R. wounded.	Wnd. 2.
PILKEM.	3.11.17	5 P.M.	Heavy shelling in neighbourhood of camp. 2. O.R. wounded on carrying party.	Wnd. 2.
LANGEMARCK	4.11.17	5 P.M.	Moved from MARSOUIN Camp into Support positions at EAGLE TRENCH, there relieving to 1/10 Liverpool R: Relief complete by 9 P.M. Casualties to day: 1 Officer wounded. (2nd Lt. J.F. Lewis: at duty.) 2. O.R. wounded.	Wnd. 1.
"	5.11.17	4 A.M.	Moved into front line at Bglé Front relieving the Liverpool R: Relief complete by 9.30 P.M. Bgde held & held (nine-scrap-Bglé Slack) Y.14.a.45.00 - Y.9.aug.13. Roles on Coy's from right to left 'A','B', 'C' & 'D' in reserve. Casualties for today: Officers nil: 2 O.R. killed. 1. O.R. wounded.	SCRAP BAZÉ supported by CARDEVOY & Wnd.
"	6.11.17	6 P.M.	To cover attack by corps. on our right, our barrage fell at 6 A.M. Heavy reply from enemy artillery. Hostile artillery also active during day and later that hour. to dechrona Track & Cramer Bn n'gunereds LOUIS Fm. Casualties: 1 Officer wounded. Lt. J.J. Jackson: 9 Other ranks killed. 21 O.R. wounded (including 2nd duty.)	Wnd. 1.
"	7.11.17	—	Heavy shelling & our artillery during day: Enemy barrage about 10-10:30 P.M. relieved by 1/10 Bn Lancashire Fusiliers. relief complete by 9.15 P.M. Casualties: 12 Other Ranks wounded. Moved into bivouacs at BOESINGHE.	Wnd.

WAR DIARY or INTELLIGENCE SUMMARY

Army Form C. 2118

November 1917.   Sheet 17.

Place	Date	Hour	Summary of Events and Information	Remarks and references to Appendices
BOESINGHE.	8.11.17	2.30 P.M.	Bn entrained for training area, at BOESINGHE STN.	Appx. 6
AUDRUICQ.	9.11.17	1. AM	Bn detrained & marched to billets at RECQUES.	Appx. 6
"	"	8.PM	Staff of 104 Other Ranks arrived from to Base.	Appx. 6
RECQUES.	13.11.17	—	Staff & G. Officers: 14 Other Ranks arrived from to Base.	Appx. 6
"	13.11.17	—	2/Lt. J. Millar. S. King Own Lancaster Regt. 2/Lt. N.R. Smith " 2/Lt. N.A. Chancellor. 4 Bn " 2/Lt. D.R. Donovan " " 2/Lt. J. A. Gordon 3/4. Spur. R. 2/Lt. 6 officers 2/Lt. G.W. Brown. 3rd Bn. R.W. Surrey R. 2/Lt. G.L. Cosgrove 1st " 2/Lt. G. Rainbow. 5th " 2/Lt. R. James. " "	learner G.G. Officers arrived Appx. 6
"	24.11.17	—	Staff & A.G. O.R. arrived from to Base. (Lt. R.C. Crow Honorbourne 2/Lt. E. Lepsing)	Appx. 6
"	30.11.17	—	Strength of Bn. 48. Officers (including L.G.s attached) 938. Other Ranks. (Nominal Roll of Officers is attached. Appendix R.	Preps attached Appx 6
	30.11.17			

W. W. Clyne Major
4. Spur. R.

2/4th Bn South Lancashire Rgt.

Appendix "R"

HEADQUARTERS.

Commanding Officer	Lt.Col. T.H.S. Marchant.
Second in Command	Major W. McClure.
A/Adjutant	Captain J. Thwaites.
Asst/Adjutant	2nd Lt. D.J. Mearns, MC
Quarter Master	Lieut. P.A. McWilliam.
Transport Officer.	Lieut. R.P. Carter.
Intelligence Officer	2nd Lt. F. Clegg.
Patrolling Officer	2nd Lt. E.L. Robinson.
Signalling Officer	Lieut. C.E. Clarkson.
Lewis Gun Officer	Lieut. G.B. Smith.
Medical Officer	Captain W.C.D. Hills. R.A.M.C.
C. of E Chaplain	Rev. W.S. Smith.
Pioneer Officer.	2nd Lt. P.O. Platts.

"A" Company.

Captain B. Milburn.
Lieut. R.B. Fairclough,
2nd Lt. J. Taylor.
2nd Lt. R. James.
2nd Lt. J.L. Lovegrove.
2nd Lt. E.W.W. Brown.

"B" Company.

Captain B. Thompson.
Lieut. H.G. Rhodes.
2nd Lt. H.L. Stevens.
2nd Lt. A. Ritchie.
2nd Lt. J.B. Gordon.
2nd Lt. J. Wilson.

"C" Company.

Captain C.G. Linnell.
Lieut. J.M. Hughes.
2nd Lt. C.J. Grierson.
2nd Lt. G. Rainbow.
2nd Lt. J.D. Fitzgerald.
2nd Lt. J.F. Tew.
2nd Lt. H.A. Smith.
2nd Lt. H.E. Chancellor.

"D" Company.

Captain R.A. Fox.
Lieut. R.C. Cross.
Lieut. A.M. Temple.
Lieut. T.D. Layland.
2nd Lt. W.L. Thompson.
2nd Lt. D.A. Duncan.

Captain J. Glascott	Attached 57th Division.
Captain S. Jepson.	Attached XI Corps.
Lieut. H.S. Sawyer.	Brigade Bombing Officer.
Lieut. A.H. Grant, M.C.,	Attached 172nd Inf.Bde.
Lieut. K.L. Gordon.	Attached 29 Prisoners of War Company.
2nd Lt. T. Molyneux.	Attached XIV Corps Reinforcement Camp.

1:10 000   K.I.

APPENDIX Q.

'C' Coy
'B' Coy
'A' Coy
'D' Coy

DISPOSITIONS
OF M Batt'n 6/11/17.

R'l Coy Platoons
L
RES
& Co HQ

X Troops on Flanks

Message Pad.

Your Message must be such as will enable the Addressee to know what the Situation is with You and your Neighbours.

NEGATIVE INFORMATION IS ALSO VALUABLE.

Strike out and alter sentences as necessary.

TO..

1. Am advancing to...
2. Am putting out (Have put out) protective parties.
3. Am sending out. Have sent out and am keeping out patrols to keep touch with the enemy.
4. Am (Have) consolidating (ed).
5. Our line now runs..
6. I require (give article or articles and number required) :—

   Send the above to...
7. Troops on my right are (give situation)

8. Troops on my left are (give situation)

9. My strength now is...
10. Am being shelled from..
11. Am held up by M.G., T.M., rifle, artillery fire from............................
12. Am now ready to...
13. Enemy line runs..
14. Enemy (strength)...................................at..............................
    doing...
15. Have captured...
16. Enemy prisoners belong to...
17. Enemy counter-attack forming up at...
18. Other remarks—

Time .... a.m. (p.m.).   Name..
Date...   Rank..
Place..   Platoon.............. Company..............
(Map Ref. or mark on back of map.)   Battalion..................................

Reference part. 3 - List of articles likely to be required -

S. A. A.   Water.
Mills No. 5 Grenades.   Rations.
Mills No. 25 Grenades.   Sandbags.
Hales No. 24 Grenades.   Screw pickets.
S. O. S.   French concertinas.
Very lights. (state kind)   Barbed wire.

Army Form C. 2118

December 1917. Sheet 18. Vol 11

WAR DIARY / INTELLIGENCE SUMMARY

(Erase heading not required.)

Instructions regarding War Diaries and Intelligence Summaries are contained in F.S. Regs., Part II. and the Staff Manual respectively. Title Pages will be prepared in manuscript.

Place	Date	Hour	Summary of Events and Information	Remarks and references to Appendices
RECQUES.	1/12/17	—	Bn in rest & training.	W.W.O.
"	6/12/17	7am	Transport moved by road to XIX Corps Reserve Area (ROUSBRUGGE) via HONDSCHOOTE; LEZ EPERLECQVE; WATOU; LEDERZEELE; RUBROUCK; WORMHOUDT; PONT DE WYLDER.	W.W.6.
"	7/12/17	4pm	Bn moved by route march to ADDINGES; thence by train to PROVEN; thence by route march to XIX Corps Reserve Area (ROUSBRUGGE) & into billets at PONT DE WYLDER.	W.W.6
WYLDER.	13/12/17	8am	Advance Party consisting of 6 Officers 30 OR. sent to ELVERDINGHE to reconnoitre LARRY CAMP	6.S.6.
"	15/12/17	9am	Inspection by GOC Brigade	6.S.6.
"	16/12/17	8am	Advance Party consisting of 1 Officer 60 OR proceeded to LARRY CAMP, ELVERDINGHE to take over	6.S.6.
"	17/12/17		Bn moved by march-route to HERZEELE; thence by train to ELVERDINGHE and into huts at LARRY CAMP.	6.S.6.
ELVERDINGHE	19/12/17	3pm	Camp shelled — 7 HV shells 1 OR wounded afterwards died in hospital	6.S.6.
"	22/12/17	10am	Commanding Officer moved forward to reconnoitre line returned 3pm.	6.S.6.
"	23/12/17	1pm	Bn moved forward into Bde Res. at BABOON CAMP. Details remaining out of line moved to HOUTMUSBOW Camp by Motor-Lorries	6.S.6.
"	24/12/17	4pm	B+D Coys moved into Front line to take over Two Companies of 2/5-S.L.R. HOUTHUIST FOREST Sector	6.S.6.
"	29/12/17	5.5pm	The enemy attacked our Front line two parties about 40 strong in all. The Left Party was dispersed immediately by our Lewis Guns & Rifle fire. Some of Right Party got to close quarters and the fight ended by Lt Temple and No2017282 Cpl Garvey after he had thrown a bomb which failed to explode bayonetting 4 killed. Casualties 4 killed 19 wounded. No2008396 S-in WILLIAMSON was killed whilst sending up SOS. Mr WO had previously been recommended for his services at LANGEMARCK & is 6th of Now and his name had been submitted for the Croix de Guerre.	+
			AVC Corps moved into the LINE B+D Coys returning to BABOON CAMP	6.S.6.
"	31/12/17		B+D Coys moved > A+C Coys moved into Line A Coy moved out to BABOON Camp	6.S.6.

J.H.S. Marchment Lt Col
2/A S Lan R.

Sheet 20.
Army Form C. 2118.

2/4 S Lanc Rgt

WAR DIARY
or
INTELLIGENCE SUMMARY.
(Erase heading not required.)

Place	Date	Hour	Summary of Events and Information	Remarks and references to Appendices
HOULTHURST FOREST SECTOR	2nd		Relieved by 7th Bn The Queens Royal West Surrey Regt. entrained BOESINGHE; Detrained INTERNATIONAL CORNER. Marched to J Camp. Divisional Report and Coy Commanders Congratulations on successful Boesin Coronetta which was taken. Killed 8 Other Ranks, Wounded 2/Lt DADMEAN (at duty) + 31 Other Ranks	R.A.T. Appendix Q R
MENEGATE CAMP	4th		Entrained INTERNATIONAL CORNER 5.0am. Detrained BAILLEUL, and marched to MENEGATE Camp. Major W. Milburn safe for Senior Officers Course Aldershot. 2nd Lt A.W. Openshaw, 2/10th Bn K.L.R. attached 2/4 S Lan R took over Company Command at Base during Lt Col YHS movements such in Hospital	R.A.T.
"	5th		Lt Col YHS Marchant returned and took over 172nd Inf Bde during Brig General G. Laynis's absence	R.A.T.
"	6th ?		Batt. part of Bde in Reserve to Bde in ARMENTIERES SECTOR.	R.A.T.
"	11-9/12/17		Working Party of 400 employed entire from ERQUINGHEM to ARMENTIERES.	R.A.T.
"	12th		201272 L/Cpl Janny and 201265 Pte J Stubbs awarded Military Medals for conspicuous gallantry in repulsing enemy raid on night 29/30 Nov. in HOULTHURST FOREST SECTOR. DRO 8/12 12.1.18	R.A.T. Appendix S
ARMENTIERES	13th		Batt. moved to Posen in Brigade Reserve at the Convent ARMENTIERES. Supplied 300 Other Ranks night Working Party Winny behind front line for 4	R.A.T.
EPINETTE SECTOR	16th 16-7/17		Batt. moved into the line taking over EPINETTE SECTOR from 2/9 Bn K.L.R	
"	18th		Relief complete 10.0 pm. Cafe R A Z awarded Military transfer for Gallantry 24/30 Oct Appendix T	DRO 17.11.15
"	19th	11.0 pm	Patrol Forward enemy machinery Target at ZILCOSE Lights as & machine guns observed.	R.A.T.
"	20th	3.0 pm	Enemy shelled Railway Embking NEJ.3030 and FOCHABER DUMP I.9.6.17 vicinity	R.A.T.
"	"	4.30 pm	East Wire Bangs fire two machines	

Sheet 2/

WAR DIARY
or
INTELLIGENCE SUMMARY.
(Erase heading not required.)

Army Form C. 2118.

Place	Date	Hour	Summary of Events and Information	Remarks and references to Appendices
EPINETTE SECTOR	21st		Relieved by 2/5 KLR relief complete 5.30 p.m., moved to Bn in Div. Reserve at MENEGATE CAMP. Casualties during tour 1 O.R. Wounded. Quiet period.	Apx Z
MENEGATE CAMP	22nd & 23rd		Supplied working party daily for Strong Points nr JESUS FARM B.26.d.31.	Apx Z
"	25th		2nd Lt. Y.H.S Marchant returned from B'ce and assumed command of B'ce.	Apx Z
EPINETTE SECTOR	27th-28th		Relieved 2/5 KLR in EPINETTE SECTOR. Relief complete 8.15 p.m.	Apx Z
"			Greater number of Minnies about JAPAN AVENUE which was at Manager's Corner Co. H.Q.	Apx Z
"	29th		One 6" Stokes fired 150 rounds, retaliation very slight.	Apx Z
"	30th		Battn relieved by 2/9 KLR relief complete 8.45 p.m. Three Coys moved into Support in Subsidiary Line, remaining Coy forming Counter Attack Reserve for the Front Line Coys. Bn HQ moved to ERQUINGHEM.	Apx Z
ERQUINGHEM	31/12		Strength 32.4.3 Officers 752 Other Ranks. Nominal roll of Officers attached. (appendix 4) Notification has been received of the forwarding of awards and Mention in the New Years Honours, Hon Major in Disp. which to Col Y.H.S M.E. J. M. Clerne, Capt. R.A. Fox Capt. Y.H.S.Marchant, Mil. Medal, the D.C.M. Private Price 202132 Sgt. J. Price.	Apx Z
			R.A. Fox Capt.	
			2/4 S. Lan. R.	

Sheet No. 21.

Army Form C. 2118.

WAR DIARY
or
INTELLIGENCE SUMMARY.
(Erase heading not required.)

2/4 S. Lan. R.

Place	Date	Hour	Summary of Events and Information	Remarks and references to Appendices
PONT NIEPPE	2.2.18		Battalion in the line relieved by the 2/8th K.L.R. and moved to Brigade in Reserve at PONT NIEPPE. Batt HQ moved ERQUINGHEM to PONT NIEPPE. Casualties during tour NIL.	R.A.F.
EPINETTE SECTOR	5.2.18	10.0pm	Relieved 2/8 K.L.R. relief complete 10.0 p.m. Tour carried on as tour previously. Barrage instead of chinese preliminary.	R.A.F.
		7.30pm	Hostile patrol of about twelve men seen near our No 2 Post. Hostile patrol again some time after dispersed on both occasions by Lewis gun fire. A force of 1 officer and 7 other ranks tried to set them off in No Mans Land, but failed to find them.	R.A.F.
	6.2.18	4.30am	Whilst descending some stairs by our No 2 Post in L.H.T. Y. Amy Sjt was [illegible] 1/c. [illegible] saw [illegible]	R.A.F.
			Situations and brought to 136 I.R. 42nd Div. Y. having stated [illegible] German accounts will be made to reach our No 2 Post by a strongpoint to Ypres they had nothing to do with the attempted Raid. They were out on a Listening Post.	
	6.2.18		Very capricious trench shelling from Enemy [illegible] between [illegible] [illegible].	appendix V
		8.30pm	Battalion in our left, after much barrage, put up many Coloured lights and we received orders from our Brigade to been Rank KILLED and 4 other Ranks wounded.	R.A.F.
WATERLANDS CAMP	8.2.18	7.45pm	Relieved by 2/10th (Scottish) K.L.R. relief complete 7.45 pm. to further casualties during relief, that was accounted for by counter batteries (Vision 2) was handed over to Artillery.	R.A.F.
			Battalion on arrival to WATERLANDS CAMP. Bath and Brigade Reserve.	
PONT NIEPPE	4.2.18		150 Other Ranks taken on the strength from 2/5 S. Lan R. (disbanded).	R.A.F.
	4.2.18		Lieut H. WEST & 2/Lt A.R. SEYMOUR transferred from 2/5 S. Lan R. posted to Bns.	R.A.F.
WATERLANDS CAMP	9.2.18		Lieut H.G. BUTLER and 2/Lt S.G. HUTTON joined Bn from 2/5 S. Lan R.	R.A.F.

Sheet No. 22

Army Form C. 2118.

WAR DIARY
or
INTELLIGENCE SUMMARY.
(Erase heading not required.)

Instructions regarding War Diaries and Intelligence Summaries are contained in F.S. Regs., Part II. and the Staff Manual respectively. Title pages will be prepared in manuscript.

Place	Date	Hour	Summary of Events and Information	Remarks and references to Appendices
WATERLANDS CAMP	10.2.15		Capt E.E. Goss USMRC reported for duty. In pre P.D. Davies R.E. Lieutenant finished trench from 2/5 S Lan R.	RA4
ERQUINGHEM	11.2.15		Bn. moved to ERQUINGHEM LAUNDRIES. Bn in Support with 1 Coy in Subsidiary Line and one at ASYLUM ARMENTIERES.	RA4
ESTAIRES	14.2.15		Lieut K.L. Yeaton struck off strength on being posted to 1/4 S Lan R.	RA4
	15.2.15		Bn was march by Route march to Divisional Reserve at ESTAIRES. 2/Lt YHS Handshaw took over temporary command of 17 & 3rd Bns. Capt RA Fox took over temporary command of 1 Bn. Capt TH Evans RAMC struck off strength on proceeding on Evacuation Leave	RA4
do	17.2.15 to 25.2.15		Unit Coys went on training for four weeks in the Corps Defences & Coy daily training Draft of 120 other ranks from 2/5 Lan R.1/9/15.	RA4
do	20.2.15		2/Lt M.D. Gayland struck off the strength on proceeding on Canadian Leave 19.2.4	RA4
do	21.2.15		2/Lt Col YHS Handshaw returned to Bn.	RA4
do	25.2.15		Strength of Bn. 43 Officers 897 other ranks. Nominal Rolls of officers attached appendix W. 2/Lt R James struck off strength of Bn on joining 1/5 L.N Lancs R 4/2/15. Notice has been received of the following detentions:— Lieut Col Yeaton 200839 CSM DC Wilkinson (Yeaton in action) Lieut de Groot 201537 Spr J. Harding	RA4 appendix W

K.A. Fox Major.
2/4 5 Lan R.

March 1918.

X-12
Sheet 23.
2/4th South Lancs Regt.
Vol 14

WAR DIARY or INTELLIGENCE SUMMARY.

Army Form C. 2118.

Place	Date	Hour	Summary of Events and Information	Remarks and references to Appendices
ESTAIRES	1/3/18		Batt. in ESTAIRES. Three Coys working on Corps Defences. One Coy training daily.	K.A.7.
"	5/3/18		G.O.C. 2 & 57th Div. inspected the Batt. in March Garden Report attached. (Appendix X).	K.A.7 Appendix X
"	9/3/18		Ordered to stand by in order to reinforce the Portuguese if attacked.	K.A.7
"	11/3/18		Batt. occupied defences (Coys) in rear of LAVENTIE for practice.	K.A.7
"	12/3/18		Draft of 60 O.R. from No.6 Entrenching Batt. Draft of 3 O.R. from Base. Lt R.P. Eastin to Hospital sick.	K.A.7
"	13/3/18		Lecture H.V. Shells in ESTAIRES. 4 other Ranks wounded. Capt E.T. Jones to 2/5 Wearing f/L and struck off strength.	K.A.7
"	14/3/18		Commanding Officer and Coy Commanders reconnoitred CORDONNERIE Sector of trenches.	K.A.7
"	15/3/18		Fine 17" Shrapnel over ESTAIRES. No casualties, nil damage.	
"	17/3/18		Draft of 5 other ranks.	K.A.7
"	19/3/18		Draft of 57 other Ranks. Lt Y.S. Laurich (US MRE) joined for Duty. 2/4 Lt L.B. Price joined the Batt.	K.A.7
CORDONNERIE SECTOR	20/3/18		Batt moved by Route March to CORDONNERIE Sector at Trenches, taking over from 9-2 B. Essex Regt. Two Coys in front + Support line, + two in Sanny Redt.	K.A.7
"	22/3/18		About 40. 77 mm shells on Support line of Right Coy area DEVON AVE.	Sketch 365W RAT.
"	24/3/18 3.0 am		2/Lt E.L. Robinson and 7 other Ranks entered enemy trenches, killing two Bosches. [illegible] indicate enemy moving Peters 4/24/3/18 (Appendix Z)(not attached) wire communication trench were in. this wire was repaired (Appendix A)(Appendix Z)	(Appendix Z) (Appendix A) K.A.7.
	4.30 am		Post L some minor gas attack. Enemy shelling.	

Army Form C. 2118.

Sheet 24

WAR DIARY
or
INTELLIGENCE SUMMARY.
(Erase heading not required)

March 1918.

Place	Date	Hour	Summary of Events and Information	Remarks and references to Appendices
CORDONNERIE SECTOR	24/3/18 (Enemy)		The remainder of the Raid was hostile and other harassing influence. Two of our men were wounded. At the same time, early fire barrage down on the flanks of the post received hitting two other ranks and wounding two other ranks. Report of Raid attached (Appendix B1)	K.at R. (Appendix B1)
	25/3/18		Draft of 13 other ranks taken on strength of Bn.	R.a.R.
RUE BIACHE	26/3/18		Relieved by 2/10 K.L.R. Relief completed 10.45 p.m. Moved to Bac in support. Came under Rue Biache. Total casualties while in line 2 O.Rs. Ranks killed, 8 other ranks wounded.	(Sheet 36 NW) R.A.R.
"	28/3/18		The area shelled by this Bn. was heavily and continuously shelled with H.E. and gas from 5.0 a.m. to 8 a.m. casualties 9 other ranks wounded, 14 other ranks N.Y.D. Gas	R.A.R.
"	30/3/18		Bn. left at 12 other Ranks joined the Bn.	R.A.R.
NEUF BERQUIN	31/3/18		Battalion relieved by 10/11th Highland Light Infantry 40th Div. Moved by route march to Brinks at NEUF BERQUIN. Strength of Bn. 45 officers 970 other ranks. Names of officers attached (Appendix C1)	R.A.R. (Appendix C1)

R.A. Fox Major.
2/4.5. Lan R.

OPERATION ORDER No.27   Copy No. 5.
by
Lieut.Colonel T.H.S. MARCHANT
commanding
2/4th Bn South Lancashire Rgt.
****

appendix V

Reference :- Sheet 36 N.W.   6/2/18.

INFORMATION 1. (a) From information obtained from prisoners taken last night, the enemy intend to attempt a raid to-night on Nos.1 or 2 Posts and his registration on No.1 Post yesterday and to-day with light T.M's, and .77 Field Guns tends to confirm this.
(b) An operation by the 171st Brigade on our left will also take place to-night according to instructions already issued, which may bring down an enemy defensive barrage on our front line.

INTENTION. 2. TO MEET (a) IN ORDER 1, O.C. RIGHT Company will make the following dispositions :-
Posts Nos.1 and 2 will be withdrawn at 6.0.pm.
Two fighting patrols, each consisting of 1 Officer and 15 Other Ranks, will operate from PEAR TREE GAP and the gap between Nos.1 and 2 Posts respectively, lying up in N.M.L. well in advance of our wire, in order that the enemy raiding parties may be surprised and rushed with the bayonet.
Vickers Guns will fire into the vacated No.2 Post and the gap between Nos.2 and 3 Posts.

TO MEET (b) IN ORDER 1. Fighting Patrols will be clear of our front line and wire before Zero hour.

3. The Right Fighting Patrol (2nd Lt. H.A. SMITH) will proceed to PEAR TREE GAP and passing through our wire will lie up about 100 yards in advance of our front line, remaining in position until the situation develops, or until dawn.
This patrol will endeavour to surprise the enemy raiding party and rush it with the bayonet. In the event of the enemy reaching No.1 Post, this patrol will cut off his retirement. In both cases it will act with the utmost determination.
On the Officer's whistle sounding all ranks will rise and charge with the bayonet.
No bombs, Lewis Gun or rifle fire will be employed.

The Left Fighting Patrol (2nd Lt. G. RAINBOW) will proceed to a point about 100 yards NORTH of No.1 Post, in the gap between Nos.1 and 2 Posts, and passing through our wire will lie up in N.M.L. about 100 to 150 yards beyond our front line.
This patrol will deal with any enemy raiding the MUSHROOM SALIENT from the south, and will therefore get into a position near the ditch leading from No.2 Post into the enemy line immediately south of the southern crater. On no account will this patrol cross to the north of this ditch. It will remain in position until the situation develops or until dawn. This patrol will endeavour to surprise the enemy and rush him with the bayonet.
In the event of the enemy reaching No.2 Post 2nd Lt. RAINBOW will :-
(a) Cut off his retirement by getting between him and his lines, or by rifle fire should the ditch in N.M.L. mentioned in the previous paragraph prevent his getting to close quarters.
(b) Send up a Green very light as a signal to the Vickers Guns in Nos.11 and 14 Posts to open fire.

ACTION OF VICKERS GUNS.	4.	The Vickers Guns at No.11 Post will be laid on the vacated No.2 Post and will open fire :- (a) 4 minutes after an enemy barrage falls on or round that post. (b) On hearing any sounds of fighting in the gap south of No.2 Post; or any movement in that post. (c) On seeing a green very light fired from N.M.L. between Nos.1 and 2 Posts (see Order 3). The Vickers Gun at No.14 Post will fire on its usual S.O.S. lines on the same occasions as No.11 Post, laid down in the previous paragraph. The O.C. Right Company will detail 1 Section to protect No.11 Vickers Gun Post, while the MUSHROOM is vacated.
LEWIS GUNS.	5.	The Lewis Gun at No.8 Post will on no account fire during the night unless it is actually attacked by the enemy at close quarters.
S.O.S.	6.	As it is intended to meet the enemy raiders by surprise and as our patrols will be operating in N.M.L., the S.O.S. should not be employed except in urgent necessity.
CODE.	7.	The following code will be used between O.C. Right Company and Battalion Headquarters :- Raid driven off - FOX. Prisoners. - THWAITES.
LIAISON.	8.	O.C. RIGHT Company will inform O.C. LEFT Company of Brigade on our right, and all posts and Trench Mortars in his sector, of his dispositions.
MISCELLAN-EOUS.	9.	Before vacating Nos.1 and 2 Posts, Very Lights will be fired and dummy sentries arranged.

(Sgd) J. THWAITES,
Captain & A/Adjutant,
2/4th Bn South Lancashire Regt.

Copy No.1. - O.C. Right Company.
     2. - O.C. Vickers Guns in
            RIGHT Company Sector.
     3. - O.C. LEFT Company.
     4. - Headquarters, 172md Inf.Bde.
     5. - Spare.

2/4th Bn South Lancashire Regt.

NOMINAL ROLL OF OFFICERS.

Role	Rank	Initials	Name
Commanding Officer.	Lt.Col.	T.H.S.	Marchant.
Second in Command.	Captain	R.A.	Fox, M.C.,
Adjutant.	Captain	J.	Thwaites.
Assistant Adjutant.	Lieut.	A.H.	Grant, M.C.,
Quartermaster.	Hon.Lt. & Q.M.	P.A.	McWilliam.
Transport Officer.	Lieut.	R.P.	Carter.
Signalling Officer.	Lieut.	C.E.	Clarkson.
Intelligence Officer.	2nd Lt.	F.	Clegg.
Patrol Officer.	2nd Lt.	E.L.	Robinson.
Lewis Gun Officer.			
Medical Officer.	Captain	E.C.	Gow.
C.of.E.Chaplain.	Captain	W.S.	SMITH.
R.C. Chaplain.	Major	P.D.	Devas.

"A" Company.

Captain B. Milburn.
Captain R.B. Fairclough.
Lieut. T. Law.
Lieut. G.B. Smith.
Lieut. H.G. Bullen.
2nd Lt. D.V. Edwards.
2nd Lt. J.L. Lovegrove.
2nd Lt. J. Taylor.

"B" Company.

Captain A. Thompson.
Lieut. N. Duncan.
2nd Lt. S.J. Milton.
2nd Lt. A. Ritchie.
2nd Lt. J.B. Gordon.

"C" Company.

Captain C.G. Linnell.
2nd Lt. C.J. Grierson.
2nd Lt. T. Molyneux.
2nd Lt. G. Rainbow.
2nd Lt. H.A. Smith.

"D" Company.

Lieut. A.M. Temple.
Lieut. R.C. Cross.
2nd Lt. D.J. Mearns, M.C.,
2nd Lt. E.W. Hodson.
2nd Lt. J. Wilson.
2nd Lt. W.L. Thompson.
2nd Lt. D.A. Duncan.

OFFICERS DETACHED FOR DUTY.

Captain J. Glascott.	Division.
Captain S. Jepson.	XI Corps.
Lieut. H.S. Sawyer.	Brigade.
Lieut. H. West.	Brigade.
2nd Lt. J.D. Fitzgerald.	Pioneer Coy.
2nd Lt. H.E. Chancellor.	L.T.M.Bty.
2nd Lt. H.L. Stevens.	Duty in ENGLAND.
2nd Lt. A.R. St.George.	Not yet joined from 2/5th S.Lan R.

SUPPLEMENT to 57th Divisional Intelligence
Summary No C 13 of 30th December 1917.

REPORT on Hostile Raid on Post V. 1, No W. on
29th December 1917.
----------- -----

Post V.1. No. 2. on our Right Battalion Sector was
being garrisoned by a platoon of the 2/4th Bn.
South Lancashire Regt., commanded by Lt TEMPLE.

At 5-15 p.m. a barrage was put down on our
Outpost Line, increasing in intendity between
5-25 and 5-40 p.m.   This was followed by a
determined raid by a party between 40 and 50
strong on V.1. No. 2 post.   The enemy advanced
in two detachments, one down the road from
V.1.a.35.00, and the other out of the Forest at
about point V.1.a.05.00.

The men in the Post held their fire and let
the Bosches get close up to them.   They then
opened fire with Lewis Gun and rifles, but the
Lewis Gun soon jammed.   The leader of the Raid
was killed by Lt. Temple when only 5 yards from
the post.   The remainder scattered, and heavy
casualties were no doubt inflicted on them by our
rifle fire, Those who got away would undoubtedly
come under heavy fire from our Barrage.

The Raid was entirely repelled by rifle fire
at short range and the Infantry were delighted
with the rapidity with which our barrage came down
and its effectiveness.

The body of the Raid Leader only has been
recovered so far, but patrols have been searching
for further identifications.

P.T.O.

The enemy's barrage was particularly accurate and heavy on our strong points and Headquarters, also on roads and track -but was inaccurate so far as our Outpost Line was concerned.

Appendix R

BRIGADE ORDERS
by
BRIGADIER GENERAL G. PAYNTER D.S.O
COMMANDING
172nd INFANTRY BRIGADE.

No 180
Monday
31/12/17.

The Corps Commander conveys his congratulations to all ranks of "D" Company "M" Battalion for their gallantry in repulsing an enemy attack on the night of the 29/30th December 1917.

        E. MARSHALL,
            Captain.
    For Brigade Major,
    172nd Infantry Brigade.

ADMINISTRATION

N I L.

        E. MARSHALL.
           Captain,
      A/Staff Captain,
   172nd Infantry Brigade.

EXTRACT FROM DIVISIONAL ROUTINE ORDERS
BY MAJOR - GENERAL R.W.R.BARNES C.B. D.S.O
COMMANDING 57th DIVISION.

Saturday, 12th January 1918.

No 201272 PTE (L/CPL) T. GARVEY, M, Bn, SOUTH LANCASHIRE REGIMENT.

At .... on the night of 29/30 December 1917, when the enemy attempted a raid on our front line under a heavy barrage, this N.C.O. showed great courage and devotion to duty. Having shot the leader of a party of the enemy, he went forward under heavy fire to gain identification from him. After the raid had been repulsed he twice went forward, still under M.G. and rifle fire, to reconnoitre and clear shell holes in front of his post of the enemy. Whilst so doing he had a personal encounter and disposed of another German. Snow was on the ground and the enemy's posts at this point are not more than 40 yards distant.

No. 201265 PTE J. STUBBS. M. BN., SOUTH LANCASHIRE REGIMENT.

At .... on the night of the 29/30 December 1917, when the enemy attempted a raid on our front line, this runner was on duty at Company Headquarters when the enemy barrage fell. The C.S.M., who was putting up the S.O.S. was killed by his side. He immediately continued the S.O.S. signals under very heavy shell fire which repeatedly struck the pill-box outside of which he was standing. He volunteered to stand outside the pill box watching for signals and for any indication of the barrage lifting, during the whole period occupied by the raid, and, after the barrage ceased, he went forward to the front line post to clear up the situation, while severe M.G. and rifle fire was in progress. His conduct throughout was admirable, and it was largely due to his courage that the S.O.S. signals were passed through.

Appendix T.

EXTRACT FROM DIVISIONAL ROUTINE ORDERS
BY MAJOR-GENERAL R.W.R.BARNES, C.B. D.S.O.
COMMANDING 57TH DIVISION.

Thursday, 17th January 1918.

CAPTAIN R. A. FOX, M. BN., SOUTH LANCASHIRE REGT.

At .... on the night of 29/30 December 1917, when the enemy attempted to rush our Lines under an intense barrage, this officer fought his Company with great skill and determination with the result that the enemy was driven off and dispersed with considerable losses before reaching our Lines, leaving identification in our hands. This Officer's capable handling of the situation and the alertness of his posts were responsible for checking and breaking up a determined rush by the enemy from the edge of the forest which, at this point, is not more than 50 yards from our Outpost Line.

Appendix C

NOMINAL ROLL OF OFFICERS

2/4TH BN SOUTH LANCASHIRE REGIMENT.

COMMANDING OFFICER	Lt.Colonel T.H.S.Marchant.
2nd IN COMMAND	Major E. G. Thin.
Adjutant.	Captain J. Thwaites.
ASST. ADJUTANT	2/Lt. D.J.Mearns M.C.
QUARTERMASTER	Hon Lt.Q.M. P.A.McWilliam.
TRANSPORT OFFICER	Lieut. R.P.Carter.
SIGNALLING OFFICER	Lieut. C.E. Clarkson.
INTELLIGENCE OFFICER	2/Lt. F. Clegg.
PATROL OFFICER	2/Lt. E. L. Robinson.
LEWIS GUN OFFICER	Lieut. T. D. Layland.
PIONEER OFFICER	Lieut. G. B. Smith.
MEDICAL OFFICER	Captain T.H.Crews (R.A.M.C).
CHAPLAIN	Rev. W. S. Smith (C.F.).

" A " COMPANY.

Captain B. Milburn.
Lieut. R. B. Fairclough.
2/Lt. J. Taylor.
2/Lt. D. V. Edwards.
2/Lt. R. James.
2/Lt. J. L. Lovegrove.

" B " COMPANY.

Captain A. Thompson.
Lieut N. Duncan.
2/Lt. H. L. Stevens.
2/Lt. A. Ritchie.
2/Lt. J. B. Gordon.
2/Lt. J. Wilson.

" C " COMPANY.

Captain C. G. Linnell.
2/Lt. C. J. Grierson
2/Lt. T. Molyneux.
2/Lt. G. Rainbow.
2/Lt. H.A. Smith.

" D " COMPANY.

Captain R. A. Fox M. C.
Lieut. A. M. Temple.
Lieut. R. C. Cross.
2/Lt. W. L. Thompson.
2/Lt. D. A. Duncan.

OFFICERS DETACHED FOR DUTY.

Captain S. Jepson	Xl Corps Headquarters.
Captain J. Glascott	57th Divisional Headquarters.
Lieut. H.S. Sawyer	172nd Infantry Brigade Headquarters.
Lieut. A.H. Grant M.C.	172nd Infantry Brigade Headquarters.
2/Lt. J.D. Fitzgerald.	172nd Brigade Pioneer Company.
2/Lt. H.E. Chancellor	172nd Brigade L.T.M.B.
2/Lt. P.O. Platts,	556 Glamorgan Field Company R.E.
2/Lt. K.L. Gordon,	29th Prisoner of War Company.

OFFICERS NOT YET POSTED TO COMPANIES.

Lieut. T. Law
2/Lt. E. W. Hodson.

2/4th Bn South Lancashire Regiment.

NOMINAL ROLL OF OFFICERS.

Appendix C.

Commanding Officer.	Lt.Col. T.H.S. Marchant.
Second in Command.	Major R.A. Fox, M.C.,
Adjutant.	Captain J. Thwaites.
Assistant Adjutant.	Lieut. A.H. Grant, M.C.,
Quartermaster.	Hon. Lt. & Q.M. P.A. McWilliam.
Transport Officer.	Lieut. R.P. Carter. (Hptl)
Act/Transport Officer.	Lieut. A.M. Temple.
Signalling Officer.	Lieut. C.E. Clarkson.
Intelligence Officer.	2/Lt. F. Clegg.
Patrol Officer.	2/Lt. E.L. Robinson.
Lewis Gun Officer.	
Medical Officer.	1st Lt. G.S. Lambeth, M.O.R.C, U.S.A.,
Chaplains – C. of E.	Captain W.S. Smith, C.F.,
R.C.	Major P.D. Devas, C.F.,

"A" Company.

Captain B. Milburn.
Lieut. T. Law.
Lieut. H.G. Bullen.
2nd Lt. D.V. Edwards.
2nd Lt. J.L. Lovegrove.
2nd Lt. J. Taylor.

"B" Company.

Captain R.B. Fairclough.
Lieut. N. Duncan.
Lieut. G.B. Smith.
2nd Lt. A. Ritchie.
2nd Lt. J.B. Gordon.   (Leave) 4/4/18.
2nd Lt. L.B. Brice.

"C" Company.

Captain C.G. Linnell.
2nd Lt. E.W. Hodson.
2nd Lt. T. Molyneux.
2nd Lt. G. Rainbow.   (Leave) 2/4/18.
2nd Lt. H.A. Smith.
2nd Lt. A.R. St.George.

"D" Company.

Lieut. R.C. Cross.
2nd Lt. D.J. Mearns, M.C.,
2nd Lt. J. Wilson.
2nd Lt. W.L. Thompson.
2nd Lt. D.A. Duncan.

OFFICERS DETACHED FOR DUTY.

Captain J. Glascott.	Division.
Captain S. Jepson.	XI Corps.
Captain A. Thompson.	Brigade Class.
2nd Lt. S.J. Milton.	-do-
Lieut. H.S. Sawyer.	Brigade.
Lieut. H. West.	
2nd Lt. J.D. Fitzgerald.	Pioneer Coy.
2nd Lt. H.E. Chancellor.	L.T.M.B.
2nd Lt. H.L. Stevens.)	Tour of duty
2nd Lt. C.J. Grierson.)	in ENGLAND.

WAR DIARY or INTELLIGENCE SUMMARY

Army Form C. 2118.

NAV. 1918.
Sheet 26.
2/4 S. Lanc. Rgt.
96R 16

Place	Date	Hour	Summary of Events and Information	Remarks and references to Appendices
NEUVE	5.5.18	2 p.m.	Bn. details moved into tents at P.H.S.; Q.M. & Transport Rear at COIGNEUX. The Bn. relieved 1/5 Bn Manchester Regt. at COUTURE COURT; relief comp. 10.30pm by 1.30am	Weu:16
COIGNEUX	6.5.18	—	Staff of 1 Offrs. Cadet (Mons.) & 4 O.R. Raw Syd Divisional Wing	Wcu 16
"	7.5.18	—	Start to I.R. Raw Syd FM Reinforcement Wing	Wcu:16
"	7.5.18	—	2/Lt. A. Mokav arrived from Base and taken on strength of Bn.	Wcu:16
GOMMECOURT	8.5.18 10.10am	Bn. in trenches & support by Ravily shelled by 4.5" & 5.9": 2 O.R. killed	Wcu 16
"	11.5.18 7.30pm–10pm	FONQUEVILLERS heavily shelled: HE & Yellow Cross Gas shells used. Transport evac. on enemy shelling. Gun Latrine (that of Offrs. Gas Casualties on the evening) & Partial lines attacked. Manchester's 2/Ayd. (Capt. R.P. Caton) x 37 O.R.	Wcu 16
"	16.5.18 9pm	GOMMECOURT heavily shelled. Sgt. Burdett & 1 R.O.R. of "D" Coy. killed & missing. Early concentration killed. EtchEq. Evacs 2 R.O.R. of "D" Coy.	Wcu:16
"	21.5.18 12.30 p.m.	Barrage put on K 1, M20 & 2. Trench Ran Bn. Transport & patrol to Trench & withdraw. 2 O.R. wounded (at duty) from A1 post	Wcu:16
"	21.5.18 10 pm	Bn. relieved by 1/6 Bn. R.W. Ramps. into billets in COIGNEUX. Relief complete by 1.15 am. Total Casualties 1 Off: 1 Offr. wounded (Gassed) 3 O.R. killed 58 O.R. wounded (incl. 40 at duty)	Wcu 16
"	25.5.18 12.0 midnight	"B" Coy. under Capt. R.B. Bridges carried out successful raid on enemy at post out West of Pigeon Wood. Sources (Mechsen's 6 at duty) Approx. 20 enemy killed & 2 machine guns captured.	Appendix "E.1" Wcu:16
COIGNEUX	17.5.18	—	Staff of 22 O.R. from Divisional Wing: Cadr. S. Haller passes to 2/4 LanC. N. & Lan. R.T. Strath at strength.	Wcu:16
"	18.5.18	—	Staff of 4 O.R. Raw Syd Divisional Wing	Wcu:16
"	28.5.18	—	COIGNEUX shelled by H.V. gun: 1 O.R. wounded. 13 Rounds fired	Wcu:16
"	29.5.18 6pm	Bn. relieved by 1/5 Bn. Loyal N. Lanc. R. and moved into Brig. Reserve at Divisional Post: Relief Comp. 12.15 am. Casualties 1 O.R. Killed 1 O.R. wounded.	Wcu:16
BIEZ WOOD	30.5.18 9–noon	Heavy bomb. of "G" & "R" areas.	Wcu:16
"	31.5.18	Strength of Offrs & Other Rs. 987 O.R. (Administrative). William W. Clarke Lieut Col. O/C 2/4 S. Lanc. R.	Appendix F.2. Wcu 16

SECRET   OPERATION ORDER No.40.   Copy No.5.
                            by
               Lieut.Colonel T.M.S.Marchant.
                     Commanding
            2/4th Bn. South Lancashire Regiment.

Reference - Map 57 D. N.E. 1/20.000.
          and aeroplane photographs.

INFORMATION. 1. A raid with Artillery support will be carried out on the
enemy trenches and C.Ts. forming the quadrilateral
between :-
          K.11.c.77.45.   K.11.c.97.55.
          K.11.c.90.35.   K.11.d.05.46.
on the night of May 25/26th.
Enemy machine guns are suspected to be at K.11.c.93.38.
and at K.11.d.02.33.

INTENTION. 2. 'B' Company (Captain FAIRCLOUGH) will carry out the raid.

The object of the raid is to :-
    (a) Obtain identification.
    (b) Kill Germans.
    (c) Bring back documentary information.
        such as letters, orders, newspapers.
    (d) Bring back Machine Guns or other armament
        which may be found.
    (e) Bomb dug-outs.

GENERAL PLAN 3. The assembly will take place a little in advance of our
OF ACTION.   front line between K.11.c.55.80 and K.11.c.70.90.

At Zero hour the Artillery will put down an intense
bombardment on the part of the enemy's trenches to be
entered, and on other selected points.

The Infantry will act as shown in diagrams in Appendix
'A'.

During the bombardment the raiding parties will move
forward as close to the barrage as safety permits.

At Zero plus 4 minutes the bombardment will lift from
the part to be entered, and parties will force an entry,
closing with the enemy with the greatest determination.

As soon as the leading parties have entered the trench
forming the 1st Objective, the rear parties will leap-
frog through and enter the Support Line trench (forming
the 2nd Objective.)

All trenches leading to the flanks and towards the enemy
will be stopped, and trenches and dugouts cleared
systematically so as to deny to the enemy the opportunity
of emerging in rear of any party.

Special Flanking parties will move forward on the Right
and Left of the leading parties to secure the flanks.
The right Flanking Party will deal with an advanced enemy
post at K.11.c.70.55.
The left Flanking party will seize and occupy the trench
junction at K.11.c.93.63. and hold it until the withdrawal of the raiding parties has taken place.

Prisoners captured will be sent back to O.C.Raid
immediately under escort.

At Zero plus 30 minutes the withdrawl will commence.
The signal will be given by whistle.

The parties raiding the 2nd Objective will be the first
to withdraw, smoke bombs being lit by the raiders to

Sheet 2.

cover their movements.

At Zero plus 31 minutes the parties in the 1st Objective will withdraw under a smoke cloud in a similar manner.

The withdrawal on the general principle laid down above, will be carried out as quickly as possible and no delay occasioned by parties waiting for individuals after the warning has been given.

On return to our lines the raiders will be directed to a sheltered position about K.10.d.80.60. to the flank of the assembly position, where they will remain until retaliation has ceased.
A tally will be taken at this place.
The raiders will be then march back by parties to the CHATEAU DE LA HAIE, where an Officer will take down particulars of the operation from each raider, and where refreshments will be provided.

DISTRIBUTION 4. O.C.Raid - Captain R.B.FAIRCLOUGH.
O.C.Right Parties 2nd Lt. J.B.GORDON.
O.C.Centre Parties. Lieutenant N.DUNCAN.
O.C.Left Parties 2nd Lt. J.WILSON.

Raid H.Q.
    Runners   4
    Telephonists   2
    Dressers & Stretcher
            Bearers. 10
                            16.

Raiding Parties.
Right Parties :-
    1st Objective.
    Sgt. GRIFFITHS and 9 O.R. - 10.

    2nd Objective.
    Sgt. O'NEILL and 17 O.R. - 18
                            28.

Centre Parties.
    1st Objective.
    L/Cpl.HAGAN and 11 O.R. - 12.

    2nd Objective.
    L/Cpl.ENTWISTLE and 9 O.R.- 10.
    Stretcher Bearers.   8
                            30.

Left Parties.
    1st Objective.
    Cpl. SMITH and 9 O.R.   - 10

    2nd Objective.
    Sgt. SMITH and 15 O.R.   - 16.
                            26.

Right Flank Party
    L/Cpl. ALBINSON & 5 O.R.   6

Left Flank Party.
    Cpl. CLOUGH & 5 O.R.   6 12.

              TOTAL 4 Offrs. 112 O.Rs.

In addition the Intelligence Officer and 8 Scouts will be employed as coverers, guides and battle stops.

P.T.O.

Sheet 3.

ASSEMBLY

5. The parties will assemble in three columns at 40 yards interval. The Intelligence Officer and his Scouts will lay out the place of assembly on a line from K.11.c.55.80. to K.11.c.70.90., and will cover the assembly and lead the raiding party on to the assembly point.
The assembly will be completed by Zero - 30 minutes.
The raiding parties will be at Raid H.Q. at Zero - 2 hours.

ORDERS FOR PARTIES.

6. (a) <u>H.Q. of O.C.Raid.</u> will be at the Company H.Q. dugout at K.11.a.22.47. where his telephonists will be in communication with Advanced Battalion H.Q. by 8.30.pm. The 2 Dressers and 8 Reserve Stretcher Bearers will be in the next deep dugout a little in rear.

(b) <u>Scouts.</u> 2nd Lt. ROBINSON and 8 Scouts will be responsible for laying out the assembly position and for observing the enemy prior to the assembly, and for covering the assembly. He will be responsible for arranging a battle stop near the point of exit from our lines to direct and assist in escorting prisoners to Raid H.Q. and to direct raiders on their return to the tally place.
As soon as the assembly is complete he will report to O.C. Raid and withdraw his Scouts (except the battle stops) to the place of tally (K.10.d.80.60)
When the withdrawal commences he will show a lamp from behind cover to direct the raiders to the tally place.

(c) <u>Right Flank Party</u> L/Cpl. ALBINSON will lead his men along the old German Front Line as near the barrage as possible, in order that he may deal with the enemy advanced post at K.11.c.70.85. at the earliest possible moment. This post must be rushed at all costs and without any hesitation. Having occupied this post he will work up the trench clearing it as he advances, and eventually gain touch with Sgt. GRIFFITHS party on the Right Flank of the 1st Objective.

(d) <u>Left Flank Party.</u> Cpl. CLOUGH will lead his party into the trench junction at K.11.c.93.63., and hold it at all costs until the raid parties have withdrawn.

(e) <u>Right Parties.</u> 2nd Lt. J.B.GORDON will himself proceed to the 2nd Objective to ensure that there is no delay in dealing with the dugouts suspected to be there.

<u>1st Objective.</u> Sgt. GRIFFITHS will clear the dugouts in the front line, sending 4 men immediately up the old German trench towards the 2nd Objective and gaining touch with the Centre Party as soon as he has cleared the dugouts and has men at his disposal.

<u>2nd Objective.</u> Sgt. O'NEILL will leap-frog through Sgt. GRIFFITHS Party, split up into two parties and act as follows :-

(i) Sgt. O'NEILL with 7 men will deal with the deep dugouts about K.11.c.82.42., sending three men to clear up the trench leading thence towards the other half of his party.
The 4 men despatched by Sgt. GRIFFITHS according to the previous para. will meet Sgt. O'NEILLS party at the dugouts.

(ii) Cpl. SAUL and 9 men will attack the suspected Machine gun at K.11.c.93.38. and form a block in the trench beyond it. He will then send 3 men to the left to gain touch with the Centre Party. The 3 men despatched by Sgt. O'NEILL to clear the trench will join Cpl. SAUL at the Machine Gun position.

P.T.O.

Sheet 4.

(f) <u>Centre Parties</u>. Lieut. DUNCAN, in addition to being in command of these parties, will from his central position be able to supervise the mopping up of the 1st Objective and the despatch of prisoners.
He will direct local operations and will have with him
  2 Runners.
  8 Stretcher Bearers.

<u>1st Objective</u>. L/Cpl. HAGAN will divide his party and will clear up the first Objective to the right and left until he gets into touch with the parties on his flanks.

<u>2nd Objective</u>. L/Cpl. ENTWISTLE will act in a similar manner.

(g) <u>Left Parties</u>. 2nd Lt. J. WILSON.

<u>1st Objective</u>. Cpl. SMITH will lead his party into the enemy trench on the left of the 1st Objective, dealing with dug-outs which are suspected to be at that point, and despatching 4 men up the trench leading towards the 2nd Objective.
  He will gain touch with the Centre Party in the 1st Objective as soon as he has cleared the dugouts and has men at his disposal.

<u>2nd Objective</u>. Sgt. SMITH will leap-frog through the 1st Objective Party and dividing will deal with a suspected machine gun and dugout with 2 parties as follows :-

(1) Sgt. SMITH with 7 men will attack the machine gun near the trench junction about K.11.d.03.53. and will detail 3 men to form a block at that point. The 4 men despatched up the trench from the 1st Objective will join Sgt. SMITH at the trench junction.

(2) Cpl. SCRUTTON with 7 men will deal with the dugout at K.11.d.05.52. and detail 3 men to form a block beyond the 2nd Objective, and when this has been done and men are available he will gain touch with the Centre party in the 2nd Objective.

(h) The Officer Commanding the Company holding the line at the point from which the raiders assemble and return will provide 2 Platoons to act in support - these platoons will be in position about K.11.a.30.75.
He has also arranged to withdraw his front line posts at the point from which the raid takes place until the operation has terminated.

ARMS & EQUIPMENT. 7. All ranks taking part will black their faces and remove all identification marks such as identity discs, regimental badges and numerals, yellow arm badges, pay books, private correspondence.
No document, map or plan is to be taken into the attack.
A label with name rank and religion, will be carried in the right breast pocket. These labels will be given up to the tally Officer on return from the raid.
No head dress will be worn.
Ammunition will be carried in the right side pocket, magazines will be charged.
Bayonets and other bright or light coloured articles will be painted a dark colour.
Articles with which individuals and parties are equipped are laid down in Appendix 'B'.
Officers will be dressed like the men.

                  P.T.O.

Sheet 5.

PASS-WORDS	8.	No pass word will be employed, but parties will inform each other of their position by calling out their leaders name which will be answered by the leader's name of other parties within hearing.
ACTION OF OTHER ARMS.	9.	Artillery - see Appendix 'C'. Machine Guns - See Appendix 'D'.

SIGNALS.	10.	(a) The withdrawal will be notified by :-
		
		    1. Reference to the watch.
		    2. Blasts by party leaders on the whistle.
		(b) A lamp will be shown at the tally place to guide the raiders to it after their return to our lines.

GENERAL INSTRUCTIONS	11.	Each party will be led by a N.C.O. and will have an Officer or senior N.C.O. in rear. The parties will act with the greatest determination and will force an entry in spite of all opposition. After the barrage lifts from the enemy front line trenches there will be no halt or pause of any kind, all parties going straight to their objectives. Bombs will only be used for dugouts and for blocking purposes. - the rifle and bayonet will be used in the trenches and in the open and must be considered the chief weapon. All prisoners must be taken immediately to O.C.Raid and not to the tally place.
RECORDS CHECKING.	12.	Major McCLURE will question all raiders and take down a narrative of the operations at the CHATEAU de la HAIE 2nd Lt. ST.GEORGE will attend the A.D.S. FONQUEVILLERS to extract information from wounded. Accurate lists of raiders will be made out by O.C.Raid one copy to be kept, and copy for Major McCLURE and one copy for 2nd Lt. ST.GEORGE.
MEDICAL	13.	Cpl.McKENZIE and Cpl. NORMAN will act as special dresser at Raid H.Q. All wounded will be brought up to them and will remain with them until all enemy retaliation has ceased. Wounded will then be evacuated to the R.A.P. GOMMECOURT.
ZERO.	14.	Zero hour will be notified later.
COMMUNICATION	15.	Battalion H.Q. will be at K.1.central. O.C.Raid will be in constant communication. For code-words see Appendix 'E'.
LIAISON	16.	An Artillery Officer will be present with O.C.Raid during the operations. He will meet O.C.Raid at Reserve Bn. H.Q. K.4.a.15.30. at 7.30.pm. May 25th.
SYNCHRONIZATION	17.	The Battn. Signalling Officer will collect all watches to be used during the operations. He will be at Right Infantry Brigade H.Q. K.1.central at 6.pm. May 25th, and synchronize watches with the Brigade Signalling Officer. He will afterwards hand them to O.C.Raid at Reserve Bn. H.Q. at K.4.a.15.30. at 7.30.pm.

                                           (Sgd) T.H.S.Marchant. Lt.Colonel.
Distribution.   Commanding 2/4th Bn.S.Lancs.R.

Copy No.1. File.
      2. O.C.Raid.
      3. Intelligence Officer.
      4. War Diary.
      5. G.O.C. 172nd Inf.Brigade.
      6.   "   171st Inf.Brigade.

SECRET.   OPERATION ORDER No.40.   Copy No. 5.
                        by
             Lieut.Colonel T.W.S. Marchant,
                       Commanding
             2/4th. Bn. South Lancashire Regiment.
             ================================

Reference - Map sh.D. S.E. 1/40,000.
            and Aeroplane Photographs.

APPENDIX D War Diary
E.I.

INFORMATION.   1. A raid with artillery support will be carried out on the
               enemy trenches and C.T.s forming the quadrilateral
               between:-
                    K.11.c.57.45.   K.11.c.67.55.
                    K.11.c.69.35.   K.11.d.05.40.
               on the night of May 29/30th.
               Enemy machine guns are suspected to be at K.11.c.93.70
               and at K.11.d.02.35

INTENTION.   2. "B" Company (Captain FAIRCLOUGH) will carry out the raid.

               The object of the raid is to:-
                    (a) Obtain identification.
                    (b) Kill Germans.
                    (c) Bring back documentary information,
                        such as letters, orders, newspapers.
                    (d) Bring back Machine Guns or other armament
                        which may be found.
                    (e) Bomb dug-outs

GENERAL PLAN   3. The assembly will take place a little in advance of our
OF ACTION.   front line between K.11.c.55.80. and K.11.c.70.80.

               At Zero hour the Artillery will put down an intense
               bombardment on the part of the enemy's trenches to be
               entered, and on other selected points.

               The Infantry will act as shown in diagrams in Appendix
               "A"

               During the bombardment the raiding parties will move
               forward as close to the barrage as safety permits.

               At Zero plus 4 minutes the bombardment will lift from the
               part to be entered, and parties will force an entry,
               closing with the enemy with the greatest determination.

               As soon as the leading parties have entered the trench
               forming the 1st. Objective, the rear parties will leap-
               frog through and enter the Support line trench forming
               the 2nd. Objective.

               All trenches leading to the flanks and towards the enemy
               will be stopped; and trenches and dug-outs cleared system-
               atically so as to deny to the enemy the opportunity of
               emerging in rear of any party.

               Special or flanking parties will move forward on the Right
               and Left of the leading parties to secure the flanks.
               The right Flanking Party will deal with an advanced
               enemy post at K.11.c.70.55.
               The left Flanking Party will seize and occupy the trench
               junction at K.11.c.93.63. and hold it until the with-
               -drawal of the raiding parties has taken place.

               Prisoners captured will be sent back to O.C. Raid
               immediately under escort.
                                                          commence.
               At Zero plus 30 minutes the withdrawal will tatevakees
               The signal will be given by whistle.

The parties raiding the 2nd Objective will be the first to withdraw, smoke bombs being lit by the raiders to cover their movements.

At Zero plus 31 minutes the parties in the 1st Objective will withdraw under a smoke cloud in a similar manner.

The withdrawal on the general principle laid down above, will be carried out as quickly as possible and no delay occasioned by parties waiting for individuals after the warning has been given.

On return to our lines the raiders will be directed to a sheltered position about K.10.d.80.60. to the flank of the assembly position, where they will remain until retaliation has ceased.
A tally will be taken at this place.
The raiders will then march back by parties to the CHATEAU DE LA HAIE, where an officer will take down particulars of the operation from each raider, and where refreshments will be provided.

DISTRIBUTION. 4.
O.C. Raid - Captain R.B. FAIRCLOUGH.
O.C. Right Parties - 2nd Lt. J.B. GORDON.
O.C. Centre Parties - Lieutenant N. DUNCAN.
O.C. Left Parties - 2nd Lt. J. WILSON.

Raid H.Q.
```
    Runners                   4
    Telephonists              2
    Dressers & Stretcher Brs 10
                                        16
```

Raiding Parties.
Right Parties :-
```
    1st Objective
    Sgt GRIFFITHS and 9 O.R.   10

    2nd Objective
    Sgt O'NEILL & 17 O.R.      18        28
```

Centre Parties.
```
    1st Objective
    L/Cpl HAGAN & 11 O.R.      12
    2nd Objective
    L/Cpl ENTWISTLE & 9 O.R.   10
    Stretcher bearers           8        30
```

Left Parties.
```
    1st Objective
    Cpl SMITH and 9 O.R.       10
    2nd Objective
    Sgt SMITH & 15 O.R.        16        26
```

Right Flank Party
```
    L/Cpl ALBINSON & 5 O.R.     6
```

Left Flank Party
```
    Cpl CLOUGH & 5 O.R.         6        12
```

TOTAL 4 Offrs, 112 O.Rs.

In addition the Intelligence Officer and 8 scouts will be employ as coverers, guides and battle stops.

ASSEMBLY. 5. The parties will assemble in three columns at 40 yds interval. The Intelligence Officer and his Scouts will lay out the place of assembly on a line from K.11.c.55.80 to K.11.c.70. & 90., and will cover the assembly and lead the parties to their positions.

The assembly will be completed by Zero - 30 minutes.
The raiding parties will be at Raid H.Q. at Zero - 2 hours.

ORDERS FOR PARTIES.
6.
(a) H.Q. of O.C. RAID. will be at the company H.Q. dugout at K.11.a.22.47. where his telephonists will be in communisation with Advanced Battalion H.Q. by 8.30 pm.
The 2 Dressers and 8 reserve Stretcher Bearers will be in the next deep dugout in a little in rear.

(b) Scouts. 2nd Lt. ROBINSON and 8 Scouts will be responsible for laying out the assembly position and for observing the enemy prior to the assembly, and for covering the assembly. He will be responsible for arranging a battle stop near the point of exit from our lines to direct and assist in escorting prisoners to Raid H.Q. and to direct raiders on their return to the tally place.
As soon as the assembly is complete he will report to O.C. Raid and withdraw his Scouts (except the battle stops) to the place of tally (K.10.d.80.60)
When the withdrawal commences he will show a lamp from behind cover to direct the raiders to the tally place.

(c) Right Flank Party. L/Cpl ALBINSON will lead his men along the old German Front Line as near the barrage as possible, in order that he may deal with the enemy advanced post at K.11.c.70.85. at the earliest possible moment. This post must be rushed at all costs and without any desitation. Having occupied this post he will work up the trench clearing it as he advances, and eventually gain touch with Sgt GRIFFITHS party on the Right Flank of the 1st Objective.

(d) Left Flank Party. Cpl CLOUGH will lead his party into the trench junction at K.11.c.93.63., and hold it at all costs until the raid parties have withdrawn.

(e) Right Parties. 2nd Lt. J.B. GORDON will himself proceed to the 2nd Objective to ensure that there is no delay in dealing with the dugouts suspected to be there.

1st Objective. Sgt GRIFFITHS will clear the dugouts in the Front Line, sending 4 men immediately up the old German trench towards the 2nd Objective; and gaining touch with the Centre Party as soon as he has cleared the dugouts and has men at his disposal.

2nd Objective. Sgt O'NEILL will leap-frog through Sgt GRIFFITHS Party, split up into two parties and act as follows :-

(i) Sgt O'NEILL with 7 men will deal with the deep dugouts about K.11.c.82.42., sending three men to clear up the trench leading thence towards the other half of his party.
The 4 men despatched by Sgt GRIFFITHS according to the previous para. will meet Sgt O'NEILLS party at the dugouts.

(ii) Cpl SAUL and 9 men will attack the suspected Machine gun at K.11.c.93.38. and form a block in the trench beyond it. He will then send 3 men to the left to gain touch with the Centre Party. The 3 men despatched by Sgt O'NEILL to clear the trench will join Cpl SAUL at the Machine gun position.

(f) Centre Parties. Lieut DUNCAN, in addition to being in command of these parties, will from his central position

be able to supervize the mopping up of the 1st Objective and the despatch of prisoners.
He will direct local operations and will have with him
  2 Runners.
  2 Stretcher Bearers.

<u>1st. Objective.</u> L/Cpl. HAGAN will divide his party and will clear up the first Objective to the right and left until he gets into touch with the parties on his flanks.

<u>2nd. Objective.</u> L/Cpl. ENTWISTLE will act in a similar manner.

(c) <u>Left Parties.</u> 2nd. Lt. J. WILSON.

<u>1st. Objective.</u> Cpl. SMITH will lead his party into the enemy trench on the left of the 1st. Objective, dealing with dug-outs which are suspected to be at that point, and despatching 4 men up the trench leading towards the 2nd. Objective.
 He will gain touch with the Centre Party in the 1st. Objective as soon as he has cleared the dug-outs and has men at his disposal.

<u>2nd. Objective.</u> Sgt. SMITH will leap-frog through the 1st. Objective Party and dividing will deal with a sus--pected machine gun and dug-out with 2 Parties as follows:-

(1) Sgt. SMITH with 7 men will attack the machine gun near the trench junction about K.11.d.05.55, and will detail 3 men to form a block at that point. The 4 men despatched up the trench from the 1st. Objective will join Sgt. SMITH at the trench junction.

(2) Cpl. COMPTON with 7 men will deal with the dug-out at K.11.d.05.52. and detail 3 men to form a block beyond the 2nd. Objective; and when this has been done and men are available he will gain touch with the Centre party in the 2nd. Objective.

(b) The Officer Commanding the Company holding the line at the point from which the raiders assemble and return, will provide 2 Platoons to act in support - these platoons will be in position about K.11.a.30.75.
 He has also arranged to withdraw his front line posts at the point from which the raid takes place until the operation has terminated.

ARMS & EQUIPMENT. 7 All ranks taking part will black their faces and remove all identification marks such as identity discs, regimental badges and numerals, yellow arm badges, pay books, private correspondence.
No document, maper plan is to be taken into the attack.
A label with name, rank and religion, will be carried in the right breast pocket. These labels will be given up to the tally officer on return from the raid.
No head-dress will be worn.
Ammunition will be carried in the right side pocket; magazines will be charged.
Bayonets and other bright or light coloured articles will be painted a dark colour.
Articles with which individuals and parties are equipped are down in Appendix "B".
Officers will be dressed like the men.

PASS-WORDS. 8. No pass word will be employed, but parties will inform each other of their position by calling out their leader's name, which will be answered by the leader's name of other parties within hearing.

ACTION OF OTHER ARMS.	9.	Artillery - See Appendix "C"
		Machine Guns - See Appendix "D"

SIGNALS. 10. (a) The withdrawal will be notified by:-

    1. Reference to the watch.
    2. Blasts by party leaders on the whistle.

(b) A lamp will be shown at the tally place to guide the raiders to it after their return to our lines

GENERAL INSTRUCTIONS. 11. Each party will be led by a N.C.O. and will have an Officer or senior N.C.O. in rear.
The parties will act with the greatest determination and will force an entry in spite of all opposition.
After the barrage lifts from the enemy front line trench there will be no halt or pause of any kind, all parties going straight to their objectives.
Bombs will only be used for dug-outs and for blocking purposes - the rifle and bayonet will be used in the trenches and in the open and must be considered the chief weapon.

All prisoners must be taken immediately to O.C.Raid and not to the tally place.

RECORDS & CHECKING. 12. Major McCLURE will question all raiders and take down a narrative of the operations at the CHATEAU de la HATE. 2nd.Lt. ST.GEORGE will attend the A.D.S., FONQUEVILLERS to extract information from wounded.

Accurate lists of raiders will be made out by O.C.Raid - one copy to be kept, and copy for Major McCLURE and one copy for 2nd.Lt. ST.GEORGE.

MEDICAL. 13. Cpl. McKENZIE and Cpl. NORMAN will act as special dressers at Raid H.Q.
All wounded will be brought up to them and woll remain with them until all enemy retaliation has ceased. Wounded will then be evacuated to the R.A.P. GOMMECOURT.

ZERO. 14. Zero hour will be notified later.

COMMUNICATION. 15. Battalion H.Q. will be at K.1.central.
O.C. Raid will be in constant communication.
For code-words see Appendix "E"

LIAISON. 16. An Artillery Officer will be present with O.C. Raid during the operations.
He will meet O.C. Raid at Reserve Battn. H.Q. K.4.a.15.30. at 7.30 p.m. May 25th.

SYNCHRONIZATION. 17. The Battn. Signalling Officer will collect all watches to be used during the operations.
He will be at Right Infantry Brigade H.Q. K.1.central at 6 p.m. May 25th and synchronize watches with the Brigade Signalling Officer. He will afterwards hand them to O.C.Raid at Reserve Battn. H.Q. K.4.a.15.30. at 7.30 p.m.

                                                     (Sgd) R.H.S.MARCHANT, Lt.Colonel;
                                                                     Commanding,
                                                                 2/4th. Bn. South Lancs. Regt

Distribution:-
Copy No.1 File.
     2 O.C.Raid.
     3 Intelligence Officer.
     4 War Diary.
     5 H.Q., 172nd. Inf.Brigade.
     6 O.C. 171st. Inf.Bde.

2/4th Bn South Lancashire Regiment.

NOMINAL ROLL OF OFFICERS.

APPENDIX: F.I.

Commanding Officer	Lt.Colonel	T.H.S.	Marchant.
Second in Command.	Major	W.	McClure.
Adjutant.	Captain	J.	Thwaites.
Asst/Adjutant.	2nd Lt.	A.R.	St.George.
Quartermaster	Hon Lt. & Q.M.	P.A.	McWilliam.
Transport Officer.	Lieut.	T.	Law.
Signalling Officer.	Lieut.	C.E.	Clarkson.
Asst/Signalling Officer	2nd Lt.	F.	Clegg.
Intelligence & Patrol Officer	2nd Lt.	E.L.	Robinson, M.C.,
Lewis Gun Officer	Lieut.	G.B.	Smith.
	~~Lieut.~~	~~A.J.~~	~~Watson.~~
Medical Officer	Lieut.	G.S.	Lambeth. U.S.M.R.C.,
C. of E. Chaplain	Captain	W.S.	Smith, C.F.

"A" Company.
****
Captain B. Milburn.
Lieut. H.G. Bullen.
2nd Lt. D.V. Edwards.
2nd Lt. J.L. Lovegrove.
2nd Lt. J. Taylor.
2nd Lt. W.O. Roberts.
Lt. A.J. Watson.

"B" Company.
****
Captain A. Thompson.
Captain R.B. Fairclough.
Lieut. N. Duncan.
2nd Lt. S.J. Milton.
2nd Lt. A. Ritchie.
2nd Lt. J.B. Gordon.
2nd Lt. L.B. Brice.
2nd Lt. J. Wilson.

"C" Company.
****
Captain C.G. Linnell.
2nd Lt. E.W. Hodson.
2nd Lt. J.D. Fitzgerald.
2nd Lt. T. Molyneux.
2nd Lt. G. Rainbow.
2nd Lt. H.A. Smith.
2nd Lt. T.S. Bryant.

"D" Company.
****
Major R.A. Fox, M.C.,
Captain T.D. Killick.
Lieut. R.C. Cross.
Lieut. A.M. Temple.
2nd Lt. D.J. Mearns, M.C.,
2nd Lt. W.L. Thompson.
2nd Lt. D.A. Duncan.

OFFICERS DETACHED FOR DUTY &c.,
****

Captain J. Glascott.	Division.
Lieut. A.H. Grant, M.C.,	"
Lieut. J. Sillivan.	Brigade.
Lieut. H.S. Sawyer.	"
Lieut. H. West.	"
2nd Lt. H.E. Chancellor.	172 L.T.M.B.
Captain R.P. Carter.	(Hospital).

INSPECTION OF BATTALIONS
by
Major-General R.W.R. BARNES, C.B., D.S.O.,
Commanding   -   57th Division.
****

The following is copy of letter received from 57th Division regarding the inspections by the Divisional Commander :-

<u>2/4th BN. SOUTH LANCASHIRE REGIMENT.</u>
       (Best Companies "B" and "D"; former
       best turned out; latter steadiest
       and handled arms best.)

"Handling of arms very good. Very steady on parade. Packs
"and turnout good. Organization of platoons very good.
"Band very smart and well turned out.
"3 rifles of the platoon inspected were dirty.
"The kits inspected were very good.
"The Transport was excellent, the Water Cart being
"exceptionally well turned out.
"Generally a very smart Battalion."

Extract from 172nd Infantry Brigade Intelligence
Summary, 24 hours ended 6.am. 24th Match, 1918.
****

4. PATROLS. Post "L" (N.5.c.80.45.) of 2/4th Bn S. Lan Rgt.
   was attacked at 4.30.am. by a hostile raiding party estimated
   between 20 and 30 strong. The attackers threw a number of
   Stick Bombs into the post and then endeavoured to rush it.
   The leader of the party, an N.C.O., was killed and other
   casualties inflicted. The remainder scattered but managed
   to take away the N.C.O's body leaving the cap with top blown
   off and his revolver. Both Lewis Guns in rear of the post
   opened fire in the gaps on the flanks.
   The attack was accompanied by a bombardment of the posts on
   either flank.
   None of our men are missing. A patrol reconnoitred No Man's
   Land but found no dead bodies.

1. Posts in N.5.c.45.25. and N.5.d.50.80. and supports in rear
   were shelled in support of raid on "L" Post.

TO :- O.C. 2/4th Bn S. Lan Rgt.   Appendix A   B.M.4670.
                                                28/3/18.

1. The Corps Commander wishes his congratulations conveyed to the Patrol Leader and his men of the 2/4th Bn South Lancs.Rgt. who carried out the successful patrol on the morning of March 24th.

2. The Divisional Commander also adds his hearty congratulations to those of the Corps Commander.

3. O.C. 2/4th Bn South Lancs.Rgt. will please convey these to 2nd Lieutenant Robinson and his men.

                                    (Sgd) C. FISHER ROWE, Captain,
                                                    Brigade Major,
                                              172nd Infantry Brigade.
28/3/18.

Army Form C. 2118/5

Sheet 27

2th Bn. S. Lan. R.

June 1918

WAR DIARY
or
INTELLIGENCE SUMMARY
(Erase heading not required.)

Instructions regarding War Diaries and Intelligence Summaries are contained in F. S. Regs, Part II. and the Staff Manual respectively. Title pages will be prepared in manuscript.

Place	Date	Hour	Summary of Events and Information	Remarks and references to Appendices
BUS WOOD	1/6/18	11 P.m.	Hostile bombardment of Bn. Hdqrs. 7 other ranks wounded & 3 or to wounded.	
	3/6/18	—	Lt. Col. H.T. Marchant, Capt. E. Maylin, Captain R.P. Catrol and Capt. T. Jackson ...	
	—	—	...	
	24/6/18	—	...	
	7/6/18	9.30 P.m.	...	
		10 P.m.	...	
	10/6/18	—	...	
		—	...	
	12/6/18	—	...	
	14/6/18	—	...	
	19/6/18	—	...	
	23/6/18	—	...	
		1.20 a.m.	...	
	25/6/18	—	...	
	30/6/18	—	...	

2/4th Bn South Lancashire Regiment.   APPENDIX. H.

NOMINAL ROLL OF OFFICERS.

Commanding Officer.	Lt.Col. T.H.S. Marchant D.S.O.
Second in Command.	Major W. McClure.
Adjutant.	Captain J. Thwaites.
Asst. Adjutant.	2/Lt. A. R. St.George.
Quartermaster.	Hon. Lt & Q.M. P. A. McWilliam.
Transport Officer.	Lieut. A. M. Temple.
Signalling Officer.	Lieut. C. E. Clarkson.
Asst. Signalling Officer.	Lieut. F. Clegg.
Intelligence & patrol Officer.	2/Lt. E. L. Robinson M.C.
Medical Officer.	1st Lt. G. S. Lambeth. MORC, U.S.A.
Chaplain, C of E.	Captain J. A. Jagoe. C.F.

"A" COMPANY.

Captain B. Milburn.
Lieut. H. G. Bullen.
Lieut. T. Law.
2/Lt. D. V. Edwards.
2/Lt. J. L. Lovegrove. (Hospital).
2/Lt. J. Taylor. (Hospital).
2/Lt. W. O. Roberts.

"B" COMPANY.

Captain A. Thompson. (Hospital).
Captain R. B. Fairclough.
Lieut. N. Duncan. M.C.
Lieut. G. B. Smith.
2/Lt. A. Ritchie.
2/Lt. J. B. Gordon.
2/Lt. J. Wilson.
2/Lt. L. B. Brice.

"C" COMPANY.

Captain C. G. Linnell M.C.
2/Lt. E. W. Hodson.
2/Lt. G. Rainbow.
2/Lt. H. A. Smith.
2/Lt. T. S. Bryant.

"D" COMPANY.

Captain T. D. Killick. (Hospital).
2/Lt. B. J. Mearns M.C.
2/Lt. W. L. Thompson.
2/Lt. D. A. Duncan.

OFFICERS DETACHED FOR DUTY.

Captain J.	Glascott.	Division.
Lieut. A. H.	Grant M.C.	"
Lieut. J.	Sullivan.	Brigade.
Lieut. H. S.	Sawyer.	"
Lieut. H.	West.	"
Lieut. A. J.	Watson.	i/c Reserve Stretcher Bearers.
2/Lt. J. D.	Fitzgerald.	252 Tunnelling Coy. R. E.

WAR DIARY or INTELLIGENCE SUMMARY

Army Form C. 2118.

July 1918.   Sheet No. 28.

Place	Date	Hour	Summary of Events and Information	Remarks and references to Appendices
GOMMECOURT WOOD	1/7/18	6 A.m	Hostile Artillery active on GOMMECOURT WOOD, & Bn position	Weld
"	2/7/18	10 P.m	Bn relieved by C/s of 1st Auckland, 3rd CANTERBURY, 2nd & 3rd Bn of NEW ZEALAND Division. Relief complete by 12.45 A.m. 3.7.18. Moved into Corps Reserve at Casualties as per list. 3 O.R. wounded. Training at ST. LEGER LES AUTHIE.	Weld
ST LEGER	5/7/18	—	Bn moved into its position in RED LINE defence system at COSNEUX. Practice & reconnaissance	Weld
"	22/7/18	—	The Bn carried out piece in all parts & to division in to conform as Moving up to Divisional Manoeuvres. C.O. Annual Division Sports held at ST LEGER	Weld
"	29/7/18	9 Am	Rail conveyed from Corps to E.N.R. Reserve. Moved by Rail to AMBRINES	Weld
SAULTY N. St ALBIN	30/7/18	—	Move by Road to area of 17th Corps area at ST AUBYN (ARRAS)	lozve
"	31/7/18	7.45 7.35	Bn moved into billets in ARRAS by route march preparatory to relieving 2 Q 18th Canadian Bn. Following Officers rejoining Bn during month of July. 2/Lt 7/18 2/Lt R.A 38. O.R. 16.7.18 2/Lt F. T. Robinson 29.7.18 Re. MAYARD 13.7.18 22. S.R. 2/Lt W. E. FOWLER 16.7.18 21.7.18 Cpl. MILL (WOODFIELD) 2/Lt J. F. NICOLL 2/Lt G. E. FOWLER 19.7.18 " 6. O.R. Strength of Bn. Lh Officers 920 O.R. Terminal Roll & Notes attached	lozle true true APPENDIX
			Will-Colonel Commdg 2/4 Bn. Kings R.	

"A" Form.
MESSAGES AND SIGNALS.
Army Form C. 2121.

APPENDIX L.1.(a)

SECRET

TO: 2/4 SLR 9KLR 1 RMF C Coy MG Bn
B Coy MG Bn 168 Bde 5 Canadian Bde
57 Div (G) 170 Inf Bde 171 Inf Bde

Sender's Number	Day of Month	In reply to Number	
BM 104	28		AAA

172 Inf Bde will attack at 12.30 PM today AAA 56 Div attack on right 2nd Canadian Div on left AAA 9 KLR will attack on right 2/4 SLR on left 1st RMF in support AAA forming up line will be on or about their front line AAA first objective U15c central – HOOD LANE sunken road in U10c 7.9 to left boundary at J10b 0.5 AAA second leading line between Bns CRUX trench with HOOD LANE AAA second objective right Bn RIENCOURT left Bn HENDECOURT AAA artillery action barrage will come down at zero on JUNO trench U13 b 8.3 trench junction U8 d 4.6 along trench to U9a 5.0 to U3c 8.7 AAA at zero + 12 minutes barrage will lift and move at rate of 200 yards in 8 minutes

MESSAGES AND SIGNALS.

"A" Form.   Army Form C. 2121.

lifting off first objective at Zero + 60 barrage will remain until Zero + 90 on line 200 yards beyond first objective AAA field art barrage will then cease AAA Heavy artillery will bombard HENDICOURT and track junctions South of it from Zero + 60 to Zero + 120 and RIENCOURT from Zero + 120 to Zero + 180 AAA

ACKNOWLEDGE

1st R.M.F will follow up the attack and Bn commanders will move forward as situation permits but will not go forward of road in U9d and a

C.F. du Rowe
O/C

From: 172 Bde
Time: 6.30 AM

SECRET

2/4 South Lancashire
Regiment

From :- The Officer Commanding,
       2/4th Bn. South Lancashire Regt.

To :- Headquarters,
       172nd Inf. Bde.

      War Diary for the month of AUGUST, 1918, enclosed.

                       William McClure
                          Major,
                       Commanding,
           2/4th Bn. South Lancashire Regt.

5/9/18.

WAR DIARY or INTELLIGENCE SUMMARY

Army Form C. 2118.

August 1918.

Sheet No. 29.
2/4 S. Lanc Regt.
Vol. 19

Place	Date	Hour	Summary of Events and Information	Remarks and references to Appendices
ARRAS	1/8/18	10 p.m.	Bn. in Reserve Barracks in ARRAS. Relieved by 1/5th Bn CAMERON INFANTRY in FRESNOY SECTOR (North Sub-Sector) Relief complete at 1 a.m.	
SABROIT in TRENCH	2/8/18	6.30	Hd.Qrs. Bn. at SABROIT TRENCH in A & B Coys. Lens Road	
	3/8/18		Bn. in same position	
	4/8/18		" " " "	
	5/8/18	2.4 pm	Enemy attempted raid on our post just right of target L. Raid repulsed.	
	6/8/18			
	17/8/18	10 p.m.	Relieved by 6th Bn Seaforth Highlanders (51st Div). Relief complete by 12.40 a.m. 18th	
	18/8/18		In L. of C. in ARRAS	
	19/8/18		" " " " 27. Commenced	
	20/8/18		Batt. marched to relief of 14/18 HUSSARS IN FRONT OF TILLOY	
	21/8/18		Batt in support line on "CRIEF" OR MUTINEUR	
	22/8/18		" " " " " " NEUVILLE	
	23/8/18	4.30	(Relief) Bn. moved to left of BOIRY TILLOY (WOZCRAVE-VE-COPPE). Bn. at BOIRY-SUR-COURT	
	24/8/18			
	25/8/18			
	26/8/18			
	27/8/18			
	28/8/18	4.30 am	Batt attacked HENDECOURT village including and trench barrage at 4.30 am. All objectives were captured. 2 Pris. 1 machine gun captured. Our casualties... 3 Coys of Cameronians relieved. B Coys. A & D Coys. Tac up position on right. 3 Coys. Cameronians S. Co's tanned 19th. Bn. arriving & remained. 20. Reserved 15 S.O. Lancs. S.	
	29.30/8	4pm	Relieved by 1/10 Hylands Bgde. Batt. moved to Xroads. Ez at HEMIN	

Army Form C. 2118.

August 1918. Sheet No. 30.

WAR DIARY
or
INTELLIGENCE SUMMARY.
(Erase heading not required.)

Instructions regarding War Diaries and Intelligence Summaries are contained in F. S. Regs., Part II. and the Staff Manual respectively. Title pages will be prepared in manuscript.

Place	Date 1918	Hour	Summary of Events and Information	Remarks and references to Appendices
HENIN.	29.	5pm	Bath. line shelled by H.V. guns; 2 O.R. wounded. 2 officers arrived from Base. Bath moved into supports in to HINDENBURG LINE near TENNER.	O.B.W.6
HINDENBURG LINE.	31.	-	Brought a Bath.' 3g officers; 715 other ranks. Received lot of officer attacks. Officers Casualties. 28.8.18. WOUNDED. Lt. E.W. HODSON. 2/Lt. T.S. BRYANT. Lt. H.C. BULLEN. 2/Lt. L.B. BRICE. 2/Lt. ARITCHIE. MISSING (I.E.E. TOWLER. (believed wounded).)	APPENDIX M.I. to W6

William W. Olivier Major
for Lt. Col. Comdg.
2nd Bn. S.W.B.

2/4 8 June R.I.
Sheet No. 29

WAR DIARY
or
INTELLIGENCE SUMMARY.

Army Form C. 2118.

(Erase heading not required.)

September 1918.

Place	Date	Hour	Summary of Events and Information	Remarks and references to Appendices
SAINDRE-BUCLIN HENNAL FONTAINE	1.	8 P.M.	Moved forward to FONTAINE. Wind & south as 2.9.18.	
	2.	8 A.M.	On attack with 148 A/T at Hyde Park & BROCOURT - QUEANT line taken. 400 prisoners & 20 machine guns captured. Officers: 2/Lt J.S. LONG, 2/Lt R.C. ROBERTS, 2/Lt L. LOVESHORE wounded in action. 2/Lt H.J. DIXON, Lt M. PHILLIPS killed in action. No other casualties in action.	
OISY COURT	3.	3 A.M.	Moved into reserve at CROISILLES. Capt T.C. 7 a.m. Bde. Bn. Capts. F. Co. ? mc MARCHANT, D.S.O. attached	
CROISILLES	8.	10.30.	Returned to B. No. 2 & to Stockade — 126 other ranks.	
TROSSY-EAU MOYENNE	9.		Returned to TROSSY-EAU MOYENNE & BDE in reserve.	
	12.	1	Moved to fight line. Gone in attd.	
	16.	1	Sans officer of T.C.R. 4 [?] with Capt. Smith killed by 10.46 Bn. Mines into	
			Training at BULLECOURT	
BULLECOURT			Remained at Training Other ranks	
BULLECOURT	21.		Moved to BAILLEULVAL by train. Bn arrived & billets for men & training.	
			Battn & Bde. from line up	
BAILLEULVAL	25.	1	At work in RIENCOURT Trn & 2 trains	
	27.	130 a.m	On line of march leaving MARILU BOYELLES. Bn. arr. RIENCOURT 2 Battalions attacked RIENCOURT near PRONVILLE. LUT Gen F. Dey attn. Military arrangements made arrival late M 7 P.M. 4 field guns 60 prisoners ? 26th Enemy captured. 2/Lt J.R.A. SMITH, 2/Lt O.F. EDWARDS, 2/Lt C. WILSON, CAPT E.G. EMSLIE, C, 2/Lt R.E. MOSS wounded in action.	
	28.	9 a.m.	Line held: On left & right. Relieved & billets in CAGNICOURT.	
			Casualties: Other ranks 2/Lt 21. Other ranks 13. B.T.E. moved in action. Co Lt Command in reserve.	
	30.	1 A.M.	Out of line. Moved into PRONVILLE F.3778d & attacking on right & left. Casualties: LIEUT D.A. DUNCAN 13 wounded; LT. H. MATTHEWS 70 T.R. wounded 3 0 R. killed. W.M. Bn.	

LT COLONEL
Commanding 2/4 Bn. 8 R.I.

2/4th Bn. South Lancashire Regiment.

APPENDIX. M2.

NOMINAL ROLL OF OFFICERS.

Commanding Officer	Lt.Col. T.H.S.Marchant, D.S.O.
Second in Command.	Major W. McClure.
Adjutant.	Captain J. Thwaites.
Assistant Adjutant.	Lieut: A.R. St George.
Quartermaster.	Hon. Lieut. & Q.M. - P.A.McWilliam.
Transport Officer.	Lieut. A.M. Temple.
Signalling Officer	Lieut. C.E. Clarkson.
Intelligence & Patrol Officer	2/Lieut. E.L.Robinson M.C.
Medical Officer.	1st Lieut: G.S. Lambeth, MORC. U.S.A.
Chaplain, C. of E.	Captain J. A. Jagoe.
Canteen Officer & i/c Stretcher Bearers.	Lieut: A. J. Watson.
Battn. Bombing Officer.	Captain J. L. Hadfield.

"A" Company.

Captain B. Milburn.
~~Lieut:~~ ~~Ellis.~~
Lieut: T. Law.
2/Lieut: D.V. Edwards.
2/Lieut: J.L. Lovegrove.
2/Lieut: W.O. Roberts.

"B" Company.

Captain R.B. Fairclough.
Lieut: N. Duncan M.C.
Lieut: G.B. Smith
2/Lieut: J.B. Gordon.
2/Lieut: J. Wilson.
2/Lieut: J.F. Nicoll.
2/Lieut: J.B.S. Davis.

"C" Company.

Captain C.G. Linnell M.C.
Lieut: G. Rainbow.
2/Lieut. J.D. Fitzgerald.
2/Lieut. H.A. Smith.
2/Lieut. J.S. Lunn.

"D" Company.

Captain D.J. Mearns M.C.
2/Lieut. W.L. Thompson.
2/Lieut. D.A. Duncan.
2/Lieut. W.L. Fowles.
2/Lieut. F.T. Robinson.

OFFICERS DETACHED FOR DUTY.

Captain J. Glascott	...	Division.
Lieut. A.H.Grant, M.C.	...	-"-
Lieut. H.S.Sawyer	...	Brigade.
Lieut. R.C.Hayward	...	-"-
Lieut. H. West.		
Lieut. J. Darrock.		

2/4th Bn. South Lancashire Regt.   APPENDIX. K.1.

NOMINAL ROLL OF OFFICERS

Commanding Officer.	Lt.Col. T.H.S. Marchant, D.S.O.
Second in Command.	Major W. McClure.
Adjutant.	Captain J. Thwaites.
Assistant Adjutant.	Lieut: A. R. St George.
Quartermaster.	Hon: Lieut: & Q.M. P.A.McWilliam.
Transport Officer.	Lieut: A. M. Temple.
Signalling Officer.	Lieut: O. E. Clarkson.
Intelligence and patrol Officer.	2/Lieut: E.L.Robinson. M.C.
Medical Officer	1st Lieut: G.S.Lambeth, MORC. U.S.A.
Chaplain, C. of E.	Captain. J. A. Jagoe.
Canteen Officer and i/c Stretcher Bearers.	Lieut: A. J. Watson.
Battn. Bombing Officer.	Captain J. L. Hadfield.

"A" Company.

Captain. B. Milburn.
Lieut: H.G. Bullen.
Lieut: T. Law.
2/Lieut: D.V. Edwards.
2/Lieut: J.L. Lovegrove.
2/Lieut: W.O. Roberts.

"B" Company.

Captain. R.B. Fairclough.
Lieut: N. Duncan M.C.
Lieut: G.B. Smith.
2/Lieut: A. Ritchie.
2/Lieut: J.B. Gordon.
2/Lieut: J. Wilson.
2/Lieut: L.B. Brice.
2/Lieut: J. F. Nicoll.

"C" Company.

Captain. C.G. Linnell M.C.
Lieut: E.W. Hodgson.
2/Lieut: J. D. Fitzgerald.
Lieut: G. Rainbow.
2/Lieut: H. A. Smith.
2/Lieut: T. S. Bryant.
2/Lieut: E. E. Towler.

"D" Company.

Captain T. D. Killick.
Captain D. J. Mearns. M.C.
2/Lieut: W. L. Thompson.
2/Lieut: D. A. Duncan
2/Lieut: W. E. Fowles.
2/Lieut: F. T. Robinson.

OFFICERS DETACHED FOR DUTY.

Captain J. Glascott.	...	Division.
Lieut: A. H. Grant. M.C.	...	-"-
Lieut: H. S. Sawyer.	...	Brigade.
Lieut: R. C. Hayward	...	-"-
Lieut: H. West.	...	
Lieut: J. Darrock.	...	

Copy Ref. B.M.131.
(Appendix P.II)

1st R.M.F.	:	172nd L.T.M.B.	:	171st Bde Left Group.
9th K.L.R.	:	A.Coy. M.G.C.	:	170th Bde Rt. Group.
2/4th S.L.R.	:	57th Divn.	:	155th Bde.
	3rd Canadian Bde.			
	1st " "			

(1) The 172nd Inf. Bde will attack to-morrow, 2/9/18 Zero hour 5 a.m. 155th Inf. Bde., 52nd Divn. is attacking on the right, and the 3rd Canadian Bde will attack on the left. Boundaries and objectives are shown on attached map. Forming-up line will be in the vicinity of Tramline in U. 11. b.

(2) The 1st R. Munster Fus. will form up first, on a one Company frontage, followed by the 2/4th S. Lancashire Regt.

(3) They will advance at Zero minus 12 behind the tanks of the Canadians, and will halt till Zero plus 30, behind the 3rd Canadian Bde, who will be formed up in front of them in U. 12.c. At Zero plus 30, they will advance along the CAGNICOURT RD (see dotted line on map attached,) and will halt where the road joins the DROCOURT-QUEANT Line, where they will obtain liaison with Lieut. Knight, in charge of half section of tanks near CALLINCARD WOOD. They will form to the right, where the CAGNICOURT ROAD crosses the DROCOURT-QUEANT TR. system, facing south on a two Battalion frontage, 2/4th S.L.R. on the right, 1st R. Munster Fus. on the left, and close up to the north-eastern edge of the CALLINCARD WOOD, where they will wait till the barrage comes down at Zero plus 90, on the line shown on attached map.

At Zero plus 90, they will advance behind the barrage and the tanks. The 2/4th S.L.R. will clear up the Western fork of the DROCOURT-QUEANT Line, and the 1st R.M.F. will clear up the eastern fork.

The 1st R.M.F. will send two platoons to occupy the spur in V.14.c. and d.

The barrage will advance at the rate of 100 yds in 5 minutes until reaching line HIPPO LANE - POSSUM LANE, where it will rest until Zero plus 135 minutes. Fire will then cease.

9th K.L.R. will take up a position by DACHSUND & GREYHOUND AV's.

The closest touch must be kept with the 3rd Canadian Bde, as this operation will not take place unless the 3rd Canadian Bde are successful in breaking through the DROCOURT-QUEANT Line.

ACTION OF M.G.s.- One Section, A. Coy., will protect the consolidation of the Munsters on the final objective, and one section will do likewise for the 2/4th Bn. South Lancs. Regt. Two sections will remain in support with 9th K.L.R. in DACHSUND AVENUE.

One Battn., 170th Bde, will clean up the TRENCH SYSTEM IN U. 24.b and d. and V. 19. a., with one Coy. M.G.s.

63rd Divn. will push through between V.27.a. 3.5. and the Northern Divn. Boundary, as soon as the objectives have been taken.

ARTILLERY ACTION.- A preparatory barrage will engage trench system V.18. V.19. V.20. until Zero plus 90., when the above barrage will sweep southwards, as described above.

HEAVY ARTILLERY.- From Zero plus 20. to Zero plus 90, H.A. will bombard V.19.a. and V. 20.c.

CONTACT AEROPLANE will call for flares at Zero plus three hours and Zero plus 5 hours, when flares will be lit and when called for.

ADV. BDE. REPORT CENTRE- U.18.c. 2.2.
  "   "   H.Q.   U. 9.a.5.0.
Rear "   "   T. 6.d.4.8.

NOMINAL ROLL OF OFFICERS.

(Appendix R.1.)

2/4th Bn. South Lancashire Regiment.

Commanding Officer.	Lieut-Colonel W. Mc Clure.
A/Adjutant.	Lieut. A. R. St George.
Quartermaster.	Hon. Lieut. & Q.M. P.A. Mc William.
Transport Officer.	Lieut. A. M. Temple.
Signalling Officer.	Lieut. C. E. Clarkson.
Canteen & Officer i/c Stretcher Bearers.	Lieut. A. J. Watson.
Medical Officer.	Lieut. G.S. Lambeth, M.C. M.R.C. U.S.A.

A. Company.

Captn. B. Milburn.
Lieut. T. Law.
2/Lieut. H.A. Roberts.
2/Lieut. A.P. Gee.
Lieut. J. Darroch, M.C.

B. Company.

Captn. J. L. Hadfield.
Captn. R.B. Fairclough. M.C.
Lieut. G.B. Smith.
2/Lieut. J.B. Gordon.
2/Lieut. J.F. Nicoll.
2/Lieut. J.B.S. Davies.
2/Lieut. J. Wilson.

C. Company.

Lieut. G. Rainbow.
2/Lieut. J.D. Fitzgerald.
2/Lieut. A. Knowles.
2/Lieut. H.L. Houghton.
2/Lieut. J.N. Huxster.

D. Company.

Captn. D. J. Mearns, M.C.
Lieut. W.L. Thompson.
2/Lieut. W.E. Fowles.
2/Lieut. F. T. Robinson.
2/Lieut. R. S. Moss.

OFFICERS DETACHED FOR DUTY.

Captn. J. Glascott.	...	Division.
Lieut. A. H. Grant, M.C.	...	-do-
Captn. J. Thwaites.	...	Brigade.
Lieut. H.S. Sawyer.	...	-do-
Lieut. R.C. Hayward.	...	-do-
Lieut. H. West.	...	-do-

(page 2.)

ACKNOWLEDGE.

                               (Sgd) C. Fisher Rowe.
                                      Captn.
                               172nd Infantry Bde.

10-15 p.m.
1st Sept. 1918.

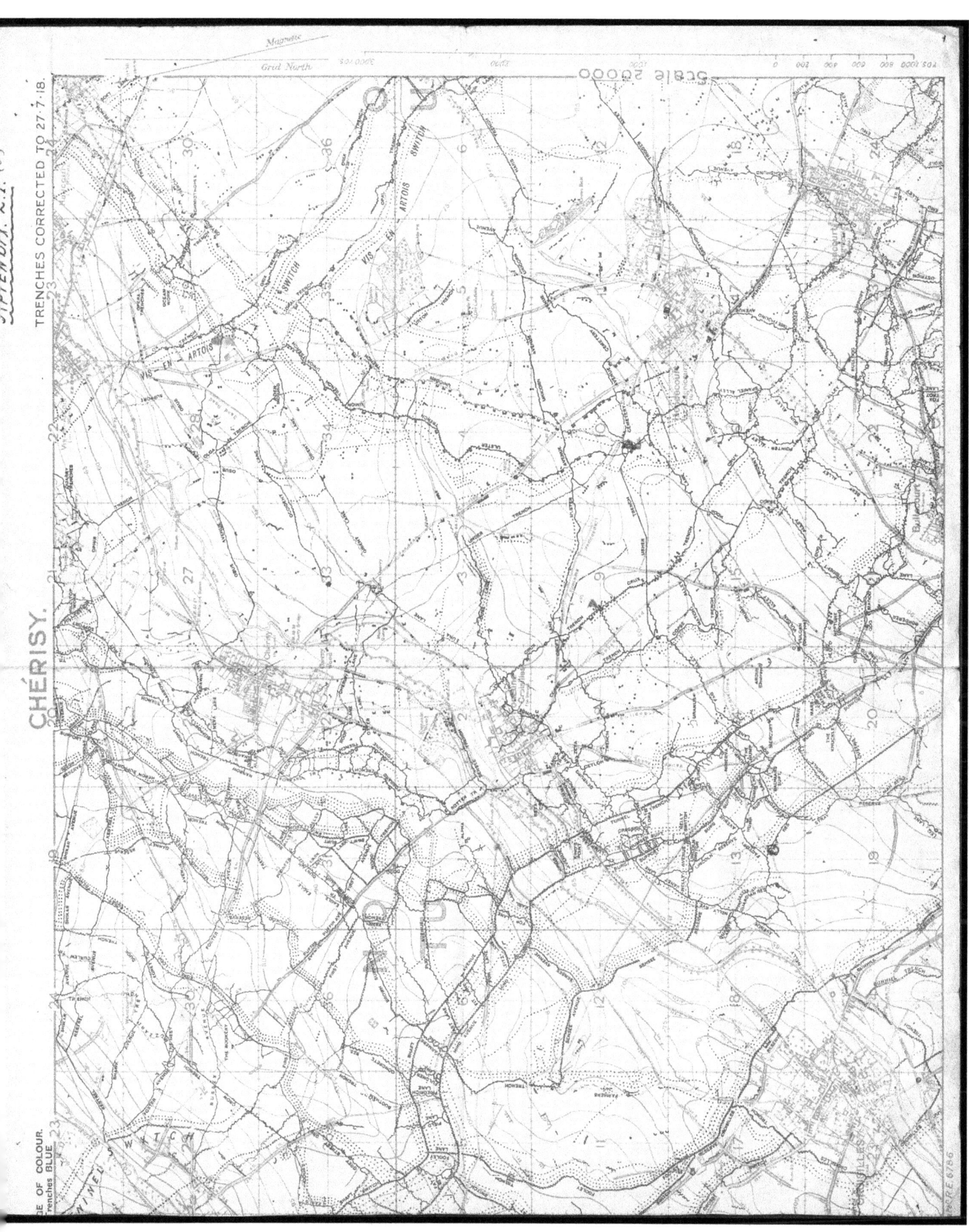

Reference Sketch on back.

To

1. My {Platoon / Company} has reached

                       (Mark position on map or give map reference).

   and is consolidating.
      has consolidated.
      is ready to advance.

2. I am (not) in touch with   on right

    and (not) with   on left.

3. I am held up at   {by wire. / by M.G. fire. / by rifle fire.

4. Enemy's artillery is firing on

              from

5. I have sent forward patrols to

6. I estimate {my casualties at / my strength at

7. I need   boxes S.A.A.
              Lewis gun drums
              Bombs
              Rifle Grenades
              Stokes Shells   (at once)
              Very Lights
              Ground Flares   (to-night)
              Stakes
              Coils wire
              Tins water
              Rations

8. I intend to

9. (General remarks on position and strength of enemy   Number of prisoners taken and identifications, if known).

            Time   Name   Rank

            Date   Platoon   Coy

                           Battalion

    Strike out all that is not applicable and forward at once to Bn. H.Q.

WAR DIARY
or
INTELLIGENCE SUMMARY

Army Form C. 2118.

(Erase heading not required)

2/4 S Lanc Regt

October 1918.

Place	Date	Hour	Summary of Events and Information	Remarks and references to Appendices
La Cl. E Nord	1/10/18	9.30 pm	En route heavily bombed by hostile aeroplanes. 2 Lt Darragh wounded. 2 OR killed. 18 OR wounded	
Burnin E - No 32 - D.M.12	2/10/18	6.30 pm	En route heavily shelled area S95 A.4.5. 3 OR killed. 23 OR wounded	
"	2/10/18	10 pm	2 Lt J Hudson wounded, proceeded to duty in few hours	
	3/10/18 6/10/18	—	12 RAM at 6.10.18. 2 Lt F.A.M. Burt & 2 Lt E.L. Combden wounded. 5 OR killed. 36 OR wounded. 6th RAMC & Civilians from Lewis Gun School, Aldershot. 12th at 33 OR. 196 killed in action. 2 OR wounded	
En Route	3 to 6.18 am		Air-Coy arrived Cogmore 11/10/18 B'de. Attended Divine Service at 11 am. Lt Rainbow, 2 Lt K.H. Ott, 2 Lt W.H. Heard joined. 2 Lts R.R. Price, W.E. Loten wounded in action. 7 OR killed, 26 OR wounded. Joined by half tread to ARELE village — MOELVRES area and beyond	
Moeuvres	9.10.18	7 pm	En route 2 Lt Kay joined. 2 Lt Bernes, 2 Lt Poll wounded in action. 3 Sergeants 2 Lt Oxton. 19 OR killed and many wounded	
Moeuvres	10/10/18	9 am	Attacked and captured line 9 N. Col. area. Road L171.k	
Wamberg	10/10/18		Moeuvres	
Ronssoy	16/10/18		Entrained Engl Hinges, India Lines in a rear area. Enemy retiring rapidly	
A Ingham	20/10/18	2.20 am	Lts Widdowson & Bowles, 2 Lts Jennings, Hall & Burton joined per L.A.E. Relief of 12/14 RQW F & F & Sergts P & Smedley Faulkner	
Lille	20.10.18		2 Lt Davis reported sick	
	20.10.18		Bn relieved 12/16 Man R under & became in Brigade Support Relief complete 3.45 pm	
	22.10.18	—		
Honnevain	24/10/18	—	Moved by Motor Lorries to Honnevain and Mont Garni. Relieved 5th Bn Ypres RL Irish LKRT. Battalion in Brigade Support. Relief complete 3.45 pm.	

WAR DIARY or INTELLIGENCE SUMMARY

October 1918 cont'd
Sheet No 31

Army Form C. 2118.

Place	Date	Hour	Summary of Events and Information	Remarks and references to Appendices
HONNEVAIN	25/10/18		Major R.A. Fox M.C. took over command of the Battalion during the Col W.H. Elgood absence on leave.	Ref.
do	27/10/18		Draft of 14 Other Ranks.	Ref.
FROYENNES	26/10/18		Relieved 9th Bn Kings (L'pool) Regt in the Front Line. Relief complete 7.45 a.m. Enemy were shelling night and ground bursts all down. 1 Other Rank Killed and 6 Other Ranks Wounded.	Ref.
do	29/10/18		Lieut J. Jones rejoined for duty, and Draft of 9 Other Ranks.	Ref.
do	30/10/18		Draft of 4 Other Ranks.	Ref.
CHERENG	31/10/18		Battalion relieved in the Line by 1/5th Bn Lond Regt (C.S.R.) 47th Div. Relief complete 6.10 p.m. Battalion marched to billets at CHERENG. Draft 2 Other Ranks. List of Honours and Immediate Rewards for recent fighting, and Descriptive Report Appendix S II on operations carried out by the Bnn on 27th, 28th, 29th Sept and 5th Oct. Appendix S III Strength of Battalion 44 Officers 705 Other Ranks. Nominal Roll of Officers	Ref. Appendix S II Appendix S III Appendix S II

R.A. Fox Major.
2/4 S Lam R.

Secret.   2/4. Bn South Lancashire Regt. Copy No

Appendix G.

Ref: Map. 57. B. N.W
         1/20000.   Operation Order No 49.   7/10/18.

1. Information

(a) The enemy is reported to be retiring on the SOUTHERN part of our THIRD ARMY front

(b) On Z day at Zero hour the XVIII Corps in conjunction with remainder of THIRD ARMY will attack and continue its advance.

(c) 170th Infantry Brigade, 57th Division, will take part in the attack, and will form a defensive flank facing NORTH to secure the left flank of the 63rd Division.

(d) 172nd Infantry Brigade will throw forward the right flank to connect with the 170th Infantry Brigade at A 27 d 2 0.

2. Intention

(a) The 2 Companies of the Battalion (A & C Companies) at present holding the line A 27 c 14 10. - A 27 c 5 8. will push their posts forward to a line approximately A 27 d 2 0 - A 27 a 5 4.
170th Brigade on the right at A 27 d 2 0. the 1st R.M.F. on the left at A 27 a 45 55

(b) D & B. Companies will remain in their present positions in Battalion reserve

3. Detail.

(a) At Zero hour the 2 RIGHT Platoons of A. Coy will go forward in one wave and get as close as possible to the barrage, following it, will take up their positions

Sheet 2.

on the new line, getting into touch with the 170th Brigade on their RIGHT, at once. The remaining platoons will follow in the usual warm formation.

(b) At the same time the two left platoons of C Company, will move forward taking up positions in the new line, and getting into touch with the post of 1st R.M.F. at A.27.a.45.53.

(c) Companies will consolidate on the new line with platoon posts chequerwise, two in the front line, two in support, and will at once consolidate. Every advantage must be taken of the tactical features of the ground on the consolidated line and of any old trenches. Gun pits, cover &c.

(d) Combined Company Headquarters will remain at the present location, A.27.c.50.42 until O/C C Company can find a new H.Qrs. suitable for his new position.

4. **Dress** FIGHTING ORDER. 5 shovels and 2 picks will be carried per platoon.

5. **Contact Aeroplane** Will call for flares at -

(a) ZERO plus 2 hours.
     ZERO - 3½ "
     ZERO - 4½ "

when forward platoons will light their flares to show their positions.

(b) A "Counter attack" plane will also be up and give the usual BROWN SMOKE signal and show wing tip lights if hostile troops

Sheet 3

are seen massing to counter attack.

6. **Barrage** There will be a Barrage of Artillery
T.M⁶ and Machine Guns.

7. **R.A.P.** As at present situated

8. A Synchronized Watch will be carried
by the bearer.

9. **Reports** To present Battalion Headquarters.

O/c A & C. Companies will make certain
the following points are reported
   (a) Capture of their objective
   (b) When 170ᵗʰ Brigade have captured
      their objective.
   (c) When they are in touch (OR NOT)
      with 170ᵗʰ Brigade ON RIGHT
   (d) When touch with 1ˢᵗ R.M.F. ON LEFT (OR NOT)

Issued by Runner   Signed Chas E. Clarkson, Lieut.
at 5.4pm   for Lieut/Adjt.
                           2/4 Bn South Lancashire Regt.

Distribution.
Copy. 1   A & C Coy.
"   2   B & D "
"   3   H.Q. 1/2 Infy Bde
"   4   H.Q. 170. " "
"   5   1ˢᵗ R.M.F.
"   6   2/4 S.Lan Rgt
"   7 & 8. War diary

Nominal Roll of Officers
joining 2/4 Bn South Lancashire Regt 23-10-18.

2/L. C. Lewis.
2/L. C. C. Evans.
2/L. I. H. Hopkins
2/L. C. H. Tranter
2/L. L. Jones.
2/L. J. Birchall
2/L. A. G. Swaddell
2/L. H. C. Shewlis.

R A Fox Major
2/4 S Lan R.

Appendix S I

2/4th Bn. South Lancashire Regt.   WAR DIARY

     APPENDIX 5a.

IMMEDIATE AWARDS - September, 1918.

BAR TO MILITARY CROSS.-

Captn. D. J. Mearns. M.C.)

MILITARY CROSS.   ) Authy:- A.R.O.s. 20. of 23/9/18.
)
Captn. R.B. Fairclough.)
Lieut. H.G. Bullen.)
Lieut. G.S. Lambeth. M.R.C. U.S.A... (Authy: A.R.O.s 24. dated 30/9/18.)

BAR TO DISTINGUISHED CONDUCT MEDAL.

200530 Sgt. Williamson T. ... Authy:- A.R.O.s 20. d/d 23/9/18.

DISTINGUISHED CONDUCT MEDAL.

202234 L/C. Taylor C. ... Authy:- A. R.O.s 20. d/d 23/9/18.

BAR TO THE MILITARY MEDAL.

40848 Pte Benson G. M.M. ... Authy:- XVII Corps. A.6/568 d/d 11/9/18

THE MILITARY MEDAL.

203069 Pte Thomason J.)
241573 Sgt Smith A.)
201678 Pte Baker W.) Authy:-
201995 Pte Hampson R.) XVII Corps. No. A.6/568 d/d 11/9/18.
241158 Pte Hornby J.)
32473 Pte McKenna P.)
200958 Pte Helsby E.)
243015 Cpl. Fairclough H.)
201685 Pte Mepham T.)
202073 L/C.Peacock T.W.)
22396 Pte Slater J.)

202256 Cpl. McKenzie J. ... Authy:- XVII Corps A.6/568. d/d 15/9/18

Appendix 5 II

2/4. Bn South Lancashire Regt.

Honours and Awards

29-10-18

201208. C.S.M. A. Kirk M.M. M.S.M.
      Awarded Bar to M.M.

241986 Pte W A Leigh. Awarded M.M.

241094 Sgt J Sill. Awarded M.M.

240484 L/Sgt J Glover (atto. L.T.M.B)
      Awarded M.M.

242015. Cpl. W. Bradbury (atto. L.T.M.B)
      Awarded M.M.

Authy: XVIII Corps. No: A6/605. of 29-10-18.

2/4th Bn. South Lancashire Regt. Appendix STI

IMMEDIATE AWARDS - September, 1918.

BAR TO MILITARY CROSS. } -

Captn. D. J. Mearns, M.C. -
"At .... during the attack on 28th Aug. 1918, after advancing 3,000 yds, this officer led his company into the village with great dash and determination, under heavy fire. When, owing to the attack on his left being held up, he found his flank seriously exposed, he showed great skill and ability in collecting parties from other companies and battalions and organising a position in trench elements on the edge of the village which he held, until relieved by fresh troops.
The losses of his Company during this attack were about 50 % and it was entirely due to his fine leading that the attack was carried through to the point reached. "

MILITARY CROSS. -

Capt. R. B. Fairclough. - "On 2nd Sept. 1918, during an attack on the .... Line near .... this officer, finding himself detached with only ten men, came in contact with a strong force of the enemy in front of his trenches. He drove this party back into the enemy trenches, and, following them up, captured 150 prisoners. He showed great courage and determination during the action and silenced an enemy machine gun which was giving great trouble to our advance. "

Lieut. H.G. Bullen. - "During the attack on 28-8-18, this officer, while in command of his Company, was wounded, being blown up by a shell at the beginning of the advance. He, however, continued to lead his men with great courage until the objective was reached. This officer set a very fine example to his men. "

Lieut. G. S. Lambeth, M.R.C. U.S.A. -

(2)

BAR TO DISTINGUISHED CONDUCT MEDAL.

200530 Sgt. Williamson T. D.C.M. - "On 28th August, 1918, during the attack on......... all officers of his Company having been wounded, this N.C.O. assumed command of the Company and reached his objective. Owing to the attack on his left flank having been held up, he formed a defensive flank and took up a position in elements of trenches he had reached, thereby protecting the left of the Battalion attack. By his good judgment and leadership, he averted the imminent possibility of a counter-attack on his left flank and was able to hold and consolidate the ground his Company had won."

DISTINGUISHED CONDUCT MEDAL.

202234 L/C. Taylor C. - " On 28/8/18, during the attack on...... this N.C.O. was in charge of a Lewis Gun team of a Company which was held up by hostile M.G. fire, at short range,,causing heavy casualties. He got together three men and rushed forward with absolute disregard of all danger, himself shooting the machine gunner and two of the enemy with his revolver, capturing three others, thereby allowing his company to reach the first objective.

After mopping up, he took up his position as left post of the line reached by the Battalion, under heavy M.G. fire from the left flank and rear and maintained his post until the Battalion was relieved."

BAR TO THE MILITARY MEDAL.)-

40848 Pte Benson, G. M.M. - "On 28-8-18, during an attack on...... this soldier, who is one of the Battalion Patrol Section, went out to search for wounded men, under heavy hostile fire. He located a number of men and went back to B.H.Q. where he took out bearer parties, and succeeded in bringing in a large number of stretcher cases. He continued this work until dusk, when all such cases had been located and the ground over which the attack had passed had been thoroughly searched."

THE MILITARY MEDAL. -

203069 Pte Thomason J. - "During the attack on 28-8-18 and 2-9-18, near.........which resulted in the capture of the..........line, this man acted as Stretcher Bearer both during both attacks and was continuously dressing and evacuating wounded under fire.

On the morning of 2-9-18, "C" and "D" Coys. of the Battalion had several casualties, including the other stretcher bearers, while going along the railway to the assembly point. Pte Thomason got these men away and caught the Company up again during the attack. Although he was the only stretcher bearer left, he got all casualties away during the day. Further, he collected prisoners who, under his command, evacuated the wounded."

241573 Sgt. Smith A. - " On the 2-9-18, near..........this N.C.O., who was Acting C.S.M. of the Coy. which was attacking the .... Line, displayed great dash and determination. The strength of the party with him, on reaching the objective, was 7, 4 being stretcher bearers. With the three armed men, he attacked three 15 of the enemy who were inflicting heavy casualties on the attacking infantry, with M.G. and rifle fire. This caused the enemy to withdraw by degrees and also kept down their fire. Later he obtained the assistance of a tank, with the aid of which, the enemy were captured - some being wounded by the fire. He also assisted the Coy. Commander in capturing 150 prisoners and a M.G."

201678 Pte Baker W. -   " In the early part of the action, he
picked up a Lewis Gun and ammunition and engaged hostile M.G.s
which were hindering the advance, causing them to cease fire, and was
responsible for the capture of 15 prisoners. After reaching the
objective, he helped to keep down hostile M.G. fire by engaging them
with his L.G.   His entire disregard of all danger from hostile
fore and the way in which he employed his gun throughout the whole
of the action, was beyond praise. "

201996 Pte Hampson R, -   " On 28-8-18, 201996 Pte Hampson R.,
32473 Pte Mc Kenna P., and 241158 Pte Hornby J. under 202234 L/C.
Taylor C.H. rushed and put out a hostile M.G. Later, under this
same N.C.O., these men took up a position as left post of the line
reached by the Battn. under heavy hostile fire. They covered the
consolidation and maintained this post until the Battalion was relieved!"

241158 Pte Hornby J. -
                              "On 28-8-18, during the attack on.........
Pte Hornby, together with No. 32473 Pte Mc Kenna P. 201995 Pte
Hampson R. under 202234 L/C. Taylor C.H. rushed and put out a hostile
M.G. Later, under this same N.C.O., Hornby with the other men named
took up a position as left post of the Line reached by the Battn. under
heavy hostile fire. They covered the consolidation and maintained
this post until the Battalion was relieved. "

32473 Pte Mc Kenna P. - "On 28-8-18, during the attack on.......
Pte Mc Kenna, together with 2o1995 Pte Hampson R, 241158 Pte
Hornby J. under 202234 L/C. Taylor C.H. rushed and put out a hostile
M.G. Later, under the same N.C.O., Mc Kenna, with the other men
named, took up a position as left post of the Line reached by the
Battn. under heavy hostile fire. They covered the consolidation
and maintained this post until the Battalion was relieved. "

200958 Pte Helsby E.   -   "On 28-8-18, during the attack on ....
this soldier went out from the Battn. Battle H.Q. to find the
advanced H.Q. and lay a line back. This he did under the heaviest
fire.   He later volunteered to go out to Coys. in the final
objective and established signal communication with B.H.Q. He set a
splendid example to the men in his section. "

243o15 Cpl. Fairclough H. - "On the 28-8-18, this N.C.O. was in the
leading wave of the attck on........ From the very start of the attack
he displayed great conrage and determination, k leading his men
forward to the objective. On reaching the objective, he gathered a
small number of men together and obtaned a L.G. Under very heavy fire,
he controlled this section, bringing his fire to bear on hostile M.G.s
which were impeding the attack, inflicting casualties on the enemy
and overcoming their resistance. The splendid example set by this
N.C.O. had a great bearing on the success of the attack. "

201685 Pte Mepham. T.   - " This man was acting as Coy.Cmmdr's
runner on 2-9-18 near...... during an attack on the ......Line.
As the platoons of the Coy. had lost direction, he went forward with
great dash and determination on to the right objective with a small
party and engaged some of the enemy who were opening heavy rifle and
M.G. fire. Later, he assisted in the capture of 150 prisoners.
Throughout the attack, this man showed great pluck and initiative. "

202073 L/C. Peacock. T.W. -   "ON 28-8-18, during an attack on......
this N.C.O. acted as runner between his C.O. and Rear H.Q. He also got
messages through to and from Coys. in the final objective under heavy
shell and M.G. fire and brought back valuable information. His
devotion to duty was the means of the progress of the attack being
reported to Bde. H.Q.

22396 Pte Slater J.   -   " On 28-8-18, during an attack on......
this soldier acted as runner to the Commanding Officer. He made
three journeys under heavy hostile shell and M.G. fire from the
Advanced Battn. H.Q. to the Battle H.Q.   He also went forward to
Coys. on the final objective, whose position was not known, under
heavy M.G. fire, carrying back messages, with an utter disregard of his
personal safety. "

202256 Cpl. McKenzie J.   -   " On 28-8-18, during the attack on.......
this N.C.O. was dressing wounded in a sunken road for 7½ hrs in the
Battn. Aid Post.   The road was heavily shelled at times, during this
period, but he remained at his post and carried out his duties in an
exemplary fashion.   It was owing to his absolute disregard of hostile
fire that so many wounded of this and other units, attacking on
the flanks, got away safely. "

2/4th Bn. South Lancashire Regt.

Appendix 5 II

Honours and Awards, 29-10-18.

BAR TO THE MILITARY MEDAL.

201208 C.S.M. H. Kirk. M.M. M.S.M. -   "During the attack on........

trench near.........on 27-9-18, his Coy. Commander having been wounded, this W.O. succeeded in taking over and re-organizing his Company.
  He carried forward the attack and killed or captured a strong enemy post which was holding up the advance.   His leadership greatly assisted the successful carrying out of the attack against strong hostile apposition.
          Later, at..........Wood, on the 2-10-18, when his Coy. Lines were heavily shelled and he was himself wounded, he remained until all the wounded of his Company had been got away and returned to Battalion from the A.D.S. when his wound had been dressed."

THE MILITARY MEDAL.

241986 Pte Leigh W.A? -   "On 27-9-18, during the attack on ......trench

in the neighbourhood of.......when all the other men in his section had been wounded, this man continued to advance, and, picking up a Lewis Gun from a wounded man, reached the furthest point of the attack where he got his gun into action against the retreating enemy.
          This man kept up his ammunition supply by jumping from shell hole to shell hole and collecting panniers from the wounded. Although wounded in the shoulder, this man continued to fire until exhausted from loss of blood. "

241 094 L/C Hill J.   -   "In the attack on ....Trench near.......

on 27-9-18, this N.C.O. finding his Coy. were held up on its left flank by heavy M.G. fire, pushed out with his team and guns and succeeded in silencing the enemy guns.   During this operation, which enabled the left to advance, the whole of his team were either killed or wounded, and he also was wounded.   His gallantry and leadership were the means of allowing our advance to continue. "

240787 L/Sgt. J. Glover. (att'd L.T.M.B.) -

  "For conspicious gallantry and devotion to duty. On the morning of 28-9-18, during the attack on.......... this N.C.O. was in charge of a 3" Stokes Mortar, supporting the 1st Bn. R.M.F.   The advance was held up by M.G. fire and this N.C.O. promptly got his gun into action in a shell hole.   He sttod out in the open, in full view of the enemy under heavy M.G. fire and coolly directed the fire of the Mortar putting the enemy M.G. and its crew out of action and enabling the advance to be continued. "

242015 Cpl. W. Bradbury. (att'd L.T.M.B.) - "On the night 27-28th

Sept. 1918, during the attack on.........this N.C.O. - commanding a L.T.M. Section in support of the South Lancs. Regt, T.F. - in the attack on ....Trench, offerred a very stubborn resistance to the enemy.
 A heavy bombing attack developed round a hostile battery position, and this N.C.O., acting on his own inititative, rushed his section well forward under very heavy M.G. fire, and opened fire at very short range on the enemy, and thus enabled out infantry to complete the capture of the position and the guns therein.   Many casualties were inflicted by this N.C.O.s prompt action. "

SECRET

Appendix S III

Ref. Map. Sheet 57c.N.E.
          1/20,000
     57b.N.W. 1/20,000   10/10/18.
     Attached Sketch Maps.

           NOTES on OPERATIONS CARRIED OUT BY THE
              2/4th Bn. SOUTH LANCASHIRE REGT
                 on 27th, 28th, and 30th Sept, 1918.
                  and 8th October, 1918.

     ATTACK ON KNAVE TRENCH, GRAINCOURT and CANTAING LINE, 27/9/18.
     ----

(1)   The Battalion left its bivouac at LAGNICOURT at 1.30 a.m.
    27th Sept and proceeded to its assembly point in the
    Hindenburg Front Line in D.16 and 17., being in position by
    4.30 a.m. Operation Order No. and nominal roll of Officers
    taking part in the operation attached.

(2)   The barrage fell at Zero Hour (5.20a.m.) and 10 minutes
    later, the Battalion was ordered to move forward to the sunken
    road D.19.d.45.75, which position was reached according to
    programme at Zero plus 90 minutes.

(3)   At this point it was found that the First Objective had
    not yet been taken by the 52nd Division and the Commanding Officer
    and Intelligence Officer went forward to the high ground
    in D.20.d. to reconnoitre. At 10.45 a.m. troops
    were seen on the high ground in E.22.b. and d. and the Battalion
    moved forward under increasingly heavy shell fire to the
    Canal crossing in E.20.d., whence it proceeded in Artillery
    formation to the high ground E.27.b.

(4)   At this point it was found that the 63rd Division were held
    up along the sunken road in E.27.b. and d. by M.G. fire
    from the Hindenburg Support line in E.28.b. and the Commanding
    Officer and Intelligence Officer went forward to reconnoitre,
    the latter being hit by M.G. fire at close range at M.27.b.7.7.
    Orders were then received from the Brigadier that the Battalion
    would remain in the area it had reached until the 63rd Division
    had recommenced the attack and made good the Hindenburg Support
    Line.

(5)   At 3.30 p.m. this attack had been launched and it succeeded
    in clearing the Hindenburg Support Line of the enemy, while
    he was also reported to be retiring from GRAINCOURT in disorder.

(6)   The Brigadier then gave verbal orders to continue the
    attack and the Battalion moved in the direction of the GRAINCOURT
    Line in K.5.c. in attack formation, being on a one Company
    frontage with Companies in the order C.D.A. and B.
    Some slight opposition was encountered from the direction of
    GRAINCOURT and there was considerable rifle fire from the same
    direction, but the advance was pushed forward to the trench
    junction at K.5.c.45.70, a few prisoners being captured
    about this point and where touch was obtained with advanced
    troops of the 63rd Division.

(7)   The attack then proceeded according to the operation orders
    and the GRAINCOURT line was all mopped up by the leading Company
    two platoons being detailed to complete the mopping up of the
    village itself. The attack proceeded satisfactorily until
    the sunken road in K.6.b. and d. was reached where the
    leading Company came under very heavy fire M.G. and rifle fire.
    Severe casualties were incurred at this point, but the attack
    continued on either side of the GRAINCOURT line, Companies
    advancing by rushes, and attempting

to cover these advances by Lewis Gun and rifle fire.
The point L.1.c.00.70. was reached by 6.30 p.m. and it
was impossible to advance further than this without encountering
further heavy losses. It was therefore decided to send one
Company on the right flank to attack the trench line in L.1.c.
L.1.d. - L.7.b., which appeared to be strongly held by the
enemy. Touch was also obtained with the 1st R.Munster Fus. on
the left flank and it was found that they were also held up by the
heavy hostile fire.

(8)   C.Company mopped up two strong German posts in KNAVE
Trench itself and by 6.50 p.m. the point L.1.c.50.60 had been
reached.

(9)   The Commanding Officer was sent for from here by the
Brigadier to the sunken road in K.6.d. and informed that he was
to make good the ground, consolidate and await orders to be issued
for an attack under a barrage, on CONTAING at dawn on the 28th
instant. After these orders had been received, B. Company
captured the trench line in L.1.d. - K.7.d., while D. Company on
the opposite flank put out of action the crews of, and
captured, two German Field guns which were firing point blank
from approximately L.1.central.
     All casualties were evacuated by 1 a.m. 28th Sept.

ATTACK ON CANTAING -- 28th September, 1918.
----

(10)   At 2.30 a.m. orders were received from the Brigade that a
barrage would fall on the CANTAING line in L.3.a. and c. at
5.30 a.m. where it would continue for 1 hour afterwards creeping
through CANTAING and falling in front of the sunken road in F.28.
a. and d. which was to be captured and consolidated as well as the
village. The 1st R.Muns. Fus. were to attack CANTAING MILL
and the strong point in F.28.a.

(11)   Owing to the determined resistance put up by the enemy
on the 27th Sept. the matter of the assembly of Companies was a
difficult one.
     A. and B. Companies were ordered to assemble in the trench
L.1.d. L.7.b. and to attack, capture and consolidate the
CANTAING line in L.3.a. and c. while C. and D. Coys. were to
assemble in KNAVE TR. in L.1.c. leap-frog through the leading
Coys. and capture CANTAING and the sunken road in F.28.d. which
they would make good.
     The attack was satisfactorily carried out and the barrage
fell at 5.30 a.m. By 6.30 a.m. A. and B. Coys had reached the
barrage mopping up several German posts on their way, and as the
barrage lifted from the CANTAING line, they rushed in, killing
or capturing a few posts which had been left. Numbers of Germans
were seen running out of this trench as the barrage lifted. C.
and D. Coys. closely following the barrage took CANTAING and the
sunken road in F.28.d. by 8.10 a.m. and consolidated on this
line. Patrols were pushed out by them to find the degree of enemy
resistance in LA FOLIE WOOD and on the east bank of the Canal
de l'ESCAUT. A. Company was then ordered to thoroughly mop up
the ~~occasional sniping shots and from~~ village of CANTAING where
trouble was being experienced from occasional sniping shots and
from one Lewis Gun. Twenty-five prisoners and several machine
guns were captured during this mopping up.
     The Battalion remained in position during the 28th and 29th
September during which the 170 Bde. had passed through them
and effected a crossing of the CANAL.

ATTACK ON PROVILLE, 30th SEPTEMBER, 1918.

(12) Orders were received at 11 p.m. on the 29th Sept. that the Battalion would pass through
  (a) 1st R. Munster Fusiliers,
  (b) 9th K. Liverpool Regt,.
who were detailed to objectives on the south suburbs of CAMBRAI, and attack squares A.12 and 18 on the 30th Sept. The Battalion moved from the village of CANTAING via the bridge at F.29.c.7.5. and reached the point F.30.a.7.4. where it was found the 1st R. Munster Fusiliers and 9th Liverpool Regt. had been held up by heavy machine gun fire on the high ground in A.20.c. A.26.a. and that the whole attack was held up by the fact that PROVILLE had not been captured.

  The Commanding Officer ordered the Battalion to advance and the leading Company to occupy the trench in A.19.d.75.10, two Companies to remain in the open behind it in Artillery formation of sections, while one Company was sent round the wooded country in A.19.b. to attempt to out-flank the strong point in the PROVILLE line in A.20.a.

(13) At 12.10, orders were received from Brigade that a barrage would fall on PROVILLE at 1 a.m. and B. Company was ordered to attack on the left of the 1st Munster Fusiliers the dividing line between Battalions being the sunken road through A.20.c. and d. and the objective being the PROVILLE line in A.20.a. b. and d. and the village itself. D. Company were to get in on the left of this line as soon as the barrage lifted. The attacking Companies got close up to the barrage and were entirely successful in their capture of the PROVILLE LINE. At the same time. the 2/7th Kings Liverpool Regt of the 171 Bde. also attacked and joined with B. Company at about A.20.a.7.3. Parties of the Battn. and of the 171 Bde. then mopped up and made good the village.

  The Battn. was relieved from this position at 3.a.m. on 1st October by the 1/5th Bn. L.North Lanc. Regt. and moved into Reserve behind LA FOLIE WOOD at F.23.a.central at 5 a.m.

ATTACK on the 8th OCTOBER, 1918.

(14) After leaving LA FOLIE WOOD, the BATTN. relieved the 6th H.L.Infantry, 52nd Div.½, on the night of the 5/6th Oct.

  On the 7th inst. orders were received that the Battn would attack the quarry and houses in A.27.central, to join up a line with the 170 Bde, who were attacking on the right with the 1st R.Royal Munster Fusiliers, who were remaining a strong point in A.27.a. as the left pivot of an attack to be made by the 3rd and 4th Armies.

(15) Orders were issued to A. and C. Coys. holding the front line to advance and conform to the new alignment, according to the attached operation order No.

(16) Companies advanced at Zero hour and as there was no barrage on our Battn front, met with severe hostile M.G. and rifle fire from the direction of FAUBOURG DE PARIS. The new line however, was captured and consolidated by 7 a.m. and touch obtained with the 170 Bde.who were attacking and had made good their objectives on our right.

  This position was we maintained until the Division was relieved on the 9th inst. At 1.30 a..,. on the 9th inst. heavy M.G. fire from the direction of the FAUBOURG, having entirely ceased, patrols were pushed out, and the houses at the fork roads A.27.b.4.3. were found occupied.

(17) Slight artillery retaliation being the only reply to the barrage for the attack of the Guards and 24th Divisions at 5.15 a.m. on this date a strong fighting patrol was pushed up to the FAUBOURG DE PARIS and this reported clear of the enemy by 6.50 a.m.

At 7.45 a.m. a patrol from our left Company gained touch with the 5th Canadian   , who were mopping up the town, near the PLACE de ARMEE in CAMBRAI and CAMBRAI was reported to be free of the enemy.

(18)　　During these operations four Field Guns, one anti-tank gun, over 150 prisoners, several L.T.M's and many machine guns besides a considerable quantity of material, were included in the captures of the Battalion,

　　　　　　　　　　　　　　　　Lieut.Colonel,
　　　　　　　　　　　　　　　　Commanding,
　　　　　　　　　　　2/4th Bn. South Lancashire Regt.

10.10.18.

Appendix XIV

Nominal Roll of Officers

2/4. Bn. South Lancashire Regt.

Commanding Officer	Lieut Col. W. McClure
2 i/c	Major R. A. Fox. M.C.
Adjt.	Lieut C. R. St George
Quartermaster	Hon Lt. & QM P. A. McWilliam
Transport Officer	Lieut C. M. Temple
Signalling Officer	Cap C. E. Clarkson
Intelligence Officer	2/Lt J. B. Gordon
Lewis Gun Officer	Lieut G. B. Smith
Canteen Officer & I/c. S. Bearer	Lieut A. J. Watson
Medical Officer	Lieut C. S. Lambert M.C.
	M.R.C.U.S.A

A. Coy

Cap. B. Milburn
Lieut S. Law
2/Lt H. A. Roberts
2/Lt R. S. Moss
2/Lt J. Wilson
2/Lt C. C. Evans
2/Lt D. Lewis

B. Coy

Cap. J. L. Sarafield
2/Lt C. H. Tranter
2/Lt J. L. Nicoll
2/Lt J. B. S. Davies
2/Lt C. E. W. Beard
2/Lt S. H. Hopkins
2/Lt S. Jones

Continued.

C. Coy

Cap R. B. Fairclough M.C.
2/L. A. Knowles
2/L. H. L. Houghton
2/L. J. W. Souster
2/L. J. Birkhall
2/L. A. C. Swaddell
Lieut. J. B. Fitzgerald

D. Coy

Cap. D. J. Kearns M.C.
Lieut W. L. Thompson
2/L. W. E. Fowler
2/L. H. L. Robinson
Lieut G. Alston
2/L. H. C. Shewlis

Officers detached for duty.

Cap. J. Glascott   Division
Lieut A. H. Grant M.C.   do.
Cap. J. Thwaite   Brigade
Lieut H. S. Sawyer   do.
Lieut R. C. Hayward M.C.   do.
Lieut H. West   do.

Lieut C. J. Grierson   Hospital.

November 1918

Army Form C. 2118.

WAR DIARY
or
INTELLIGENCE SUMMARY
(Erase heading not required)

Place	Date	Hour	Summary of Events and Information	Remarks and references to Appendices
CHERENG	1/11/18		Moved to Rest Billets at FAUBOURG DE FIVES, LILLE.	
LILLE	11/11/18		Armistice with Germany signed at 5.0 am. Hostilities ceased at 11.0 am.	
"	12/11/18		Capt J. M. Short T.F.C.E. reported for attachment.	
"	13/11/18		Lt Col W Ing. McK returned and took over command of Battalion.	
"	15/11/18		Battalion Inspection by Divisional Commander. Before the Inspection attacked Appendix T1. Battalion formed guard of honour under command of Capt J. McNamee M.C. to General Sir H. Horne, Commander-in-chief of the Allied armies, on his visit to 5th Army H.Q. The Guard of honour was first inspected by Lt General Burchwood 5th Army Commander, and afterwards by General Sir H. Horne attended by General Marechal Foch. Speech of Marechal Foch and nominal Role of Guard of Honour attached.	Appendix T1 Appendix T2 RMZ
"	19/11/18		Lieut F.J. Jackson joined Bn for duty.	RMZ
"	29/11/18		2nd Lt R.W. Hodson joined Bn for duty.	RMZ
"	30/11/18		The following Award has been made during the month 29781 Pte Jackson H awarded Military Medal. The following Drafts have reported during the month (6.O.R. 4/11/18)(6.O.R. 14/11/18)(3.O.R 15/11/18)(18.O.R 20/11/18)(5.O.R 21/11/18)(6.O.R 22/11/18)(6.O.R 22/11/18)(7.O.R 26/11/18)(5.O.R 29/11/18). 33 Other Ranks admitted to Hospital Sick during month. Strength of Battalion 42 Officers 793 Other Ranks. Nominal Role of Officers attached	Appendix T3 RMZ Appendix T4

R A Lot Major
2/4 S. Lan R

Appendix T

NOTES ON INSPECTION OF 172nd INF. BDE
BY G.O.C.

	OTHER RANKS.			TRANSPORT.		
				TURN OUT.		
	Turnout.	Steadiness.	March past.	Horses.	Vehicles.	Harness.
1st Bn R. Muns Fus.	Poor.	Satisfactory	V. Fair.	Poor.	Good.	Bad.
9th Bn L'pool Regt.	V.Poor.	"	Good.	Good.	Good.	Good.
2/4th Bn S.Lan.Regt.	V.Good.	"	Good.	Good.	Good.	Good.
172nd L.T.M.Bty.	Good.	"	Good.	Good.	Good.	Good.

H. Rutbun,
Captain,
a/Brigade Major,
172nd Inf. Bde.

14/11/3.

NOTICE.

The following is published for communication to all ranks.

"On 15th November Marshal FOCH honoured the Fifth Army by visiting the Army Headquarters. In the course of his remarks the Marshal said:-

> I have come to offer my congratulations and thanks to you and to the men of your Army for the great works achieved and the glorious results obtained in the last few days. We have won the victory by our tenacity and by the firm resolve of every man to continue fighting until victory was assured. Some of your Divisions were tired Divisions who had fought in great battles on other parts of the Front, but, under your leadership, they never faltered. They advanced at the side of your fit men. Your soldiers continued to march when they were exhausted, and they fought, and fought well, when they were worn out. It is with such indomitable will that the war has been won. At the moment of ceasing hostilities the enemy troops were demoralized and disorganized, and their lines of communication were in a state of chaos. Had we continued the war for another fortnight we might have won a most wonderful and complete military victory. But it would have been inhuman to risk the life of one of our soldiers unnecessarily. The Germans asked for an armistice, we renounced the certainty of further military glory and gave it to them. I am deeply sensible of the fact that Lille was delivered without damage to the Town, and I am grateful for the help given so generously to the inhabitants. This time my visit is short, but I intend to come back. I want to see your men, and I want to speak to them of the glorious deeds that the British Army has achieved".

NOMINAL ROLL OF OFFICERS AND OTHER RANKS OF THE 2/4th BN
SOUTH LANCASHIRE REGIMENT WHO FORMED THE GUARD OF HONOUR
TO MARSHAL FOCH ON 15th NOVEMBER 1918.

Captain D. J. Mearns M.C.
Lieut. G. Alston M.M.
2/Lieut J. Wildon.

202224	Pte	Andrews	E.	43873 Pte Archer	H.
45760	Pte	Burgess	F.	241456 Pte Crompton	J.
241605	L/C	Costello	J.	241150 Cpl Deacle	J.
45616	Pte	Dickinson	F.	242493 Pte Eden	D.
241914	Pte	French	F.	202957 L/Cpl Foy	R.
13644	Pte	Gilbert	A.	200589 Sgt Harper	T.A.
18161	Pte	Jones	T.	242239 L/C Jameson	T.
202142	Pte	Lythgoe	J.	202635 Pte Lowe	A.
32943	Pte	Minshull	G.	202158 Ogden	W.
32938	Pte	Quilliam	H.	242143 Pte Stevens	A.
50644	Pte	Schofield	A.	32940 Pte Sutton	A.
32936	Pte	Sandbach	J.W.	44118 Pte Tomlinson	F.
202199	Pte	Welsby	E.	201612 Pte Wood	T.A.
240346	L/C	Speake	F.	46033 Pte Greenhill	A.
29885	Pte	Twigg	E.	26387 Pte Bonney	W.
44205	Pte	Dennison	S.A.	31746 L/C Albinson	J.
32919	Pte	Robertson	W.	240652 Sgt Parry	J.R.
13159	Pte	Parr	J.	240804 Pte Jones	E.
242697	Pte	Gleaver	N.	202051 Pte Catterall	R.
240140	Pte	Feeney	T.	201680 Pte Boon	J.
201544	L/C	Brimelow	E.A.	13524 Pte Martin	T.
241937	Pte	Sergeant	W.	241128 Pte Ashton	J.
201573	Pte	Evans	H.	32903 Pte Hall	F.
265996	Pte	Lund	J.	201787 Pte Bibby	J.
202922	Pte	Bates	H.	202939 Pte King	T.
200879	L/C	Smith	T.	201498 Pte Peel	J.J.
202207	Pte	Mannion	F.	40962 Pte James	E.B.
44096	Pte	Spence	T.	16007 Sgt Tracey	J.
240978	Cpl	Dutton	W.	202883 Cpl Brooking	W.
34136	Cpl	Graff M.M.	P.	241926 Cpl Barrett	J.
32401	L/C	Sexton	H.	241195 L/C Smith	J.
241964	Pte	Makin	H.	240377 Pte Houghton	W.
202232	Pte	Oakes	J.	200583 Pte Worsley	J.
31899	Pte	Harrop	J.	34171 Pte Begg	R.
201089	Pte	Monks	R.	240883 Pte Lyons	R.
240842	Pte	Corns	H.	31963 Pte Hodgson	I.
32407	Pte	Tilbury	R.	13954 Pte Lewis	H.
242135	Pte	Bridge	A.	242745 Pte Cooper	G.B.
241980	Pte	Stone	A.E.	242162 Pte Large	H.
201455	Pte	Watkins	E.	1479 Pte Glynn	W.
13315	Sgt	Rhodes	T.H.	31889 Cpl Houghton	A.
202842	L/C	Hackney	T.	37279 L/C Caunter	R.
43132	L/C	Dean	E.W.	240758 L/C Brophy	T.
31124	Pte	Smith	G.	202223 Pte Forster	T.
40947	Pte	Haycock	D.M.	241965 Pte McGuire	P.
45976	Pte	Thomas	R.E.	241182 Pte Byrom	W.
242287	Pte	Gibbons	T.	202235 Pte Parr	A.
240376	Pte	Johnson	A.	241157 Pte Pickavance	J.
18737	Pte	Turner	J.C.	241091 Pte Williams	P.
241905	Pte	Dunn	T.	37480 Pte Turton	F.
32594	Pte	Spoors	R.	39090 Pte Brunt	G.
241916	Pte	Conway	P.	46117 Pte Wynn	J.
202261	Pte	Tomlin	H.	240691 R.S.M. Roughley	J.
40848	Pte	Benson M.M.	G.		

Appendix T 3

HONOURS AND AWARDS.

The Field Marshall Commanding-in-Chief has, under authority delegated to him, awarded the MILITARY MEDAL to the undernamed:-
(Authority:- M.S./H/11886 dated 18/11/18).

No. 29781. Pte H. COOKSON, South Lancashire Regiment (T.F.).

"This soldier has been a Battalion runner during the past twelve months and has done exceptionally well in his duties.
During the period under review and more especially in the attacks carried out by the Battalion on 28/8/18 and 2/9/18 this runner has carried messages under heavy shell-fire and rifle fire between Battalion Headquarters and Advanced Headquarters, and also from the latter to the forward Companies.
He is most trustworthy and reliable and has always shown an utter disregard for his personal safety when delivering a message.
He set a very fine example to all runners by the way he carried out his duties".

2/4th Bn SOUTH LANCASHIRE REGIMENT.

Appendix T

NOMINAL ROLL OF OFFICERS.

Commanding Officer,	Lt-Col. W. McClure.
2nd in Command.	Major R. A. Fox M.C.
A/Adjutant.	Lieut A. R. St. George.
Quartermaster.	Lieut P. A. McWilliam.
Transport Officer.	Lieut. A. N. Temple.
Signalling Officer.	Captain C.E. Clarkson.
Asst. Signalling Officer.	2/Lieut J.B.S. Davis.
Intelligence Officer.	2/Lieut. J. B. Gordon.
Lewis Gun Officer.	Lieut. G. B. Smith.
Canteen Officer.	Lieut. A. J. Watson.
Medical Officer.	Lieut G. S. Lambeth M.C. M.R.C. U.S.A.
Chaplain, C of E.	Captain J. M. Short.

"A" COMPANY.

Captain B. Milburn.
Lieut. T. Law.
Lieut. G. Alston M.M.
2/Lieut H. A. Roberts.
2/Lieut. R. S. Moss.
2/Lieut J. Wilson.
2/Lieut C. C. Evans.
2/Lieut D. Lewis.

"B" COMPANY.

Captain J. L. Hadfield.
2/Lieut C. H. Tranter.
2/Lieut J. F. Nicoll.
2/Lieut A.E.W. Beard.
2/Lieut T. H. Hopkins.
2/Lieut T. Jones.

"C" COMPANY.

Captain R. B. Fairclough M.C.
Lieut F. T. Jackson.
Lieut. J. D. Fitzgerald.
2/Lieut A. Knowles.
2/Lieut H. L. Houghton.
2/Lieut J. N. Huxter.
2/Lieut J. Birchall.
2/Lieut A. C. Twaddell.

"D" COMPANY.

Captain D. J. Mearns M.C.
Lieut W. L. Thompson.
2/Lieut W.E. Fowles.
2/Lieut F. T. Robinson.
2/Lieut H. C. Thewlis.

OFFICERS DETACHED FOR DUTY.

```
Captain  J.      Thwaites.           172nd Infantry Brigade.
Lieut.   R. C.   Hayward M.C.          -    do    -
Lieut    H.      West                  -    do    -
Lieut.   E. W.   Hodson.             Not yet posted to Company).
```

WAR DIARY
or
INTELLIGENCE SUMMARY.

(Erase heading not required.)

December 1918.

Army Form C. 2118.

2/4 South Lancashire

Place	Date	Hour	Summary of Events and Information	Remarks and references to Appendices
Froid LILLE	3/12/18		Batt. moved by march route to BOIS L'EPINOY and were accommodated in Huts.	R/17
BOIS L'EPINOY	4/12/18		Batt. marched through the devastated area via LENS to MARŒIL near ARRAS and moved into temp Hutments.	R/17
MARŒUIL	7/12/18		Lt H.L Stevens rejoined on leave for duty after my months tour of Duty in England.	R/17
MARŒUIL	9/12/18		Bates inspected by Brig Gen J. Kaymer DSO commanding 172nd Inf Bde	R/17
do	9/12/18		Draft and Chance of 9 other Ranks.	R/17
do	10/12/18		2 6 Other Ranks "Miners" to Base for transfer to Dispersal Area.	R/17
"	14/12/18		Draft and Chance of 14 Other Ranks. 2 6 Other Ranks "Miners" to Base for transfer to Dispersal Area.	R/17
"	13/12/18		1 5 Other Ranks "Miners" to Base for transfer to Dispersal Area.	R/17
"	14/12/18		6 Other Ranks "Miners" to Base for transfer to Dispersal Area.	R/17
"	15/12/18		10 Other Ranks "Miners" to Base for transfer to Dispersal Area.	R/17
"	18/12/18 to 23/12/18		3 Other Ranks "Miners" to Base for transfer to Employment Dispersal Area. 6 Other Ranks Draft and Tradesmen.	R/17
"	25/12/18		Capt A.T.T. Storey joined the Batten from Duty.	R/17
"	26/12/18		2 Other Ranks "Young Service" to Base for transfer to Dispersal Area.	R/17
"	29/12/18		2 Lt J.H.S. Hilton joined the Batten for Duty.	R/17
"	30/12/18		100 men sent out communication salvaging area North of ARRAS	R/17
"	31/12/18		30 Other Ranks ex communication salvaging area North of ARRAS	R/17

Army Form C. 2118.

December 1915   Sheet 34

WAR DIARY
or
INTELLIGENCE SUMMARY.

(Erase heading not required.)

Instructions regarding War Diaries and Intelligence Summaries are contained in F. S. Regs., Part II. and the Staff Manual respectively. Title pages will be prepared in manuscript.

Place	Date	Hour	Summary of Events and Information	Remarks and references to Appendices
MARDEUIL	3/12/15		Colm. Rank turned to Vicech, and Lieut. Rank myself owing to a fire breaking out in a Drug Case while exchanging Edo B. Milner was mentioned in Despatches (New Years List) 28/12/15 Capt A.M. Storey mentioned in Despatches (New Years List) 28/12/15	
		No 24053 Sergt M Rafferty mentioned in Despatches (New Years List) Younis 25/12/15	App: A1
		Strength of March — 42 Officers 715 other Ranks.	

R.N. Fox Major.
2/4 S. Lan R.

Appendix 2

Extract from 172nd Infantry Brigade Intelligence
Summary, 24 hours ending 6.am. 24th March, 1918.
****

5A. PATROLS.

2nd Lieut. E.L. ROBINSON and 7 O.R.(2/4th Bn S. Lan Rgt.) left our lines at N.10.b.39.40. as a fighting patrol at 2.15.am. and entered the enemy's lines at N.10.b.55.15. 2nd Lieut. ROBINSON and 2 O.R. then entered the enemy's trench leaving the remainder of the patrol outside the gap in the wire. They proceeded along NEEDLE TRENCH in a N.E. direction to a point N.16.b.76.30. Two efforts were made to get to the support line, but owing to the state of the ground this was found to be impossible. Horse transport, a train, and a working party were heard about N.10.d.central The support line appeared to be unoccupied, and no sounds or Very Lights came from it. On return to the point of entrance to the enemy's trench, the patrol was challanged twice, a stick bomb was thrown and two revolver shots fired. 2nd Lieut. ROBINSON and the 2 O.R. immediately fired, killing two Germans. Identifications from post cards found on one of the bodies shows 370 I.R. (Normal). No casualties were sustained by our Patrol.

57th Division
172nd Infantry Brigade

WAR DIARY

2/4th BATTALION

THE SOUTH LANCASHIRE REGIMENT

APRIL 1918

WAR DIARY or INTELLIGENCE SUMMARY

APRIL 1918

Army Form C. 2118.

Place	Date	Hour	Summary of Events and Information	Remarks and references to Appendices
NEUF BERQUIN	1.4.18		MAJOR W. McCLURE (returned from Senior Officers School ALDERSHOT) & draft of 30 O.R. taken on strength.	
	2.4.18	2 P.M.	Moved by route march into billets at LE PARC (NIEPPE FOREST)	Attd.
NIEPPE FOREST LE PARC	3.4.18	11 P.M.	Entrained at STEENBECQUE, detrained at DOULLENS; bivouaced by road march & billets at BEAUDRICOURT. Sgt. W. HATTON: Pte J. STEWART awarded to Military Medal.	APPENDIX A Lotter 10
BEAUDRICOURT	4.4.18	6 P.M.	Moved by route march & billets at SOMBRIN.	Lotter 10
SOMBRIN	8.4.18	9 A.M.	Moved by route march to billets at MARIEUX accordance.	Lotter 10
MARIEUX	9.4.18	—	Draft of 20 O.R. per base. 2/Lt E.L. Robinson awarded to Military Cross.	APPENDIX B Lotter 10
	10.4.18	—	Draft of 1 Officer (Capt. J.E. CHALLEN) arrived from 2/S. LAN. R. 2 O.R. from base	Lotter 10
	11.4.18	3 P.M.	Bivouac by route march to billets at WARLOZEL	Lotter 10
WARLOZEL	12.4.18	6 P.M.	Proceeded by route march & Camps in Copse N.W. of HENU	Lotter 10
HENU	14.4.18	—	Draft of 29 O.R. from base	Lotter 10
	16.4.18	—	Moved into Camps in Wood N.E. of HENU	Lotter 10
	15.4.18	—	Working parties on RED LINE Afternoon. Sgt W. DOE to Army Reserve.	Lotter 10
	20.4.18		RED LINE. Corps Line. Cosseux. Sebastre. Bienvillers.	Lotter 10
	25.4.18	—	Draft of 3 Officers (Capt. T.S. REDDY: 2/Lt W. ROBERTS: 2/Lt T.S. BRYANT.) & 33 O.R. from base.	Lotter 10
			2/Lt PORTER rejoined from hospital.	
	29.4.18	—	Bn. inspected by II Corps Commander, Lt General Sir C.W. JACOB, K.C.B., D.S.O.	Lotter 10
	30.4.18	—	Strength of Bn. 47 Officers and 1040 O.R. Nominal List of Officers attached	APPENDIX D. Lotter 10

J.K.N. Marshall
Lt. Colonel
Cmdg 2/4 Bn. South Lancashire Regt.

2/4th Bn. South Lancashire Regiment.   Appendix "D".

NOMINAL ROLL OF OFFICERS.

Commanding Officer	Lt.Col. T.B. Marchant.
Second in Command.	Major C. McClure.
Adjutant.	Captain J. Thwaites.
Asst/Adjutant.	2/Lt. A.F. St.George.
Quartemaster	Hon Lt. & QM R.A. McMillan.
Transport Officer.	Lieut. T.F. Carter.
Asst/Transport Officer.	Lieut. A.E. Temple.
Signalling Officer.	Lieut. G.E. Clarkson.
Asst/Signalling Officer.	2/Lt. F. Clegg.
Intelligence & Patrol Officer	2/Lt. R.B. Robinson M.C.,
Lewis Gun Officer.	Lieut. C.B. Smith.
Medical Officer.	1st Lt. D.S. Lambeth.
	M.R.C.,USA.
Chaplains - C. of E.	Captain R... Smith, C.F.,
R.C.	Major F.B. Dovan, C.F.,

"A" Company.

Captain G. Milburn.
Lieut. E. Law.
Lieut. R.H. Dillon.
2nd Lt. F.V. Edwards.
2nd Lt. J.A. Lovegrove.
2nd Lt. J. Taylor.
2nd Lt. W.E. Roberts.

"B" Company.

Captain A. Knappan.
Captain R.B. Fairclough.
Lieut. R. Duncan.
2nd Lt. J.C. Hilton.
2nd Lt. A. Ritchie.
2nd Lt. J.H. Gordon.
2nd Lt. J.B. Price.
2nd Lt. J. Wilson.

"C" Company.

Captain O.S. Linnell.
2nd Lt. G.H. Hodson.
2nd Lt. J.D. Fitzgerald.
2nd Lt. T. Molyneux.
2nd Lt. G. Rainbow.
2nd Lt. H.A. Smith.
2nd Lt. T.S. Bryant.

"D" Company.

Major R.A. Fox, D.S.O.,
Captain T.C. Killion.
Lieut. R.G. Green.
2nd Lt. D.J. Morris, D.C.M.,
2nd Lt. R.L. Thompson.
2nd Lt. D.A. Duncan.

OFFICERS DETACHED FOR DUTY.

Captain J.C. Challen.	XV Corps F. & B. Camp.
Captain J. Glascott.	Division.
Lieut. A.B. Grant, M.C.,	
Lieut. J. Sullivan.	Brigade.
Lieut. H.S. Sawyer.	
Lieut. R. West.	"
2nd Lt. R.S. Chancellor.	170 L.T.M.B.

Appendix "E".

Extract from 57 Divisional Routine Orders d/d 31/3/18.

539. HONOURS AND REWARDS.

The Corps Commander has, under authority granted by His Majesty the King, awarded the Military Medal to the undernamed. (Athy :- XV Corps Nos.A.C.9218/7 and A.C.9218/8, dated 29th March, 1918.)

201428. Sergt. W. HATTON, "M" Battn.

For bravery on the night of March 23rd/24th, 1918, whilst reconnoitring ground between the enemy's front and support line in the.......... Sector, with an Officer and a man.

The party was fired on and attacked in the German Trenches. Fire was immediately opened and two Germans were killed. The party at once took the identifications off the dead men and returned to our lines.

This N.C.O. showed great courage and initiative during the episode and ably assisted the Officer.

32393, Pte J. STEWART, "M" Battn.

This man volunteered to accompany an Officer and a N.C.O. to reconnoitre the enemy's trenches in the...........Sector on the night of March 23rd/24th, 1918.

Whilst returning from examining the ground between the Front and Support Line the party was fired on and attacked.

In the fight which ensued two Germans were killed and identifications were collected from the bodies.

Throughout Private STEWART acted with the greatest gallantry.

Appendix "F".

Extract from 57th Divisional Routine Orders d/d -7/4/18.

348. HONOURS and REWARDS.

The Field Marshall Commanding-in-Chief has, under authority granted by His Majesty the King, awarded the MILITARY CROSS to the undernamed. (Athy - MS/H/8516 of 3/4/18).

2nd Lieut. E.L. ROBINSON, "M" Bn. South Lancs Regt.

On the night of March 23rd/24th 1918, in the ....Sector this Officer led a patrol of 1 N.C.O. and 1 man into the enemy trenches.

Whilst returning from a reconnaissance of the ground between the enemy's Front and Support Line they were fired on and attacked. Lieutenant ROBINSON and the two men immediately opened fire and killed two of the enemy. All identifications were then taken off the bodies.

Owing to his gallant conduct, valuable information was secured and a very fine example of patrol work was set for all ranks.

2/4th BN SOUTH LANCASHIRE REGIMENT Appendix A.

NOMINAL ROLL OF OFFICERS.

Commanding Officer.	Lt. Col. W. McClure.
2nd in Command.	Major R.A. Fox M.C.
A/Adjutant.	Captain G.E. Clarkson.
Asst. Adjutant.	Lieut. A.R. St. George.
Quartermaster.	Lieut. P.A. McWilliam.
Transport Officer.	Lieut. A.M. Temple.
Signalling Officer.	2/Lieut. J.B.S. Davis.
Demobilization Officer.	Lieut. J.B. Gordon.
Canteen Officer.	Lieut. A.J. Watson.
Intelligence Officer.	Captain A.T.T. Storey.
Medical Officer.	Lieut. G.S. Lambeth M.C. M.R.C. U.S.A.
Chaplain. C of E.	Captain J.M. Short.

"A" COMPANY.

Captain N. Milburn.
Lieut. T. Law.
Lieut. G. Alston M.M.
2/Lieut H. A. Roberts.
2/Lieut R. S. Moss.
2/Lieut J. Wilson.
2/Lieut. C. C. Evans.
2/Lieut D. Lewis.

"B" COMPANY.

Captain J. L. Hadfield.
Lieut. H. L. Stevsn.
2/Lieut. A.E.W. Beard.
2/Lieut. J. F. Nicoll.
2/Lieut. T. Jones.
2/Lieut. C.H. Tranter.
2/Lieut. T. H. Hopkins.

"C" COMPANY.

Lieut. E. W. Hodson.
Lieut. F. I. Jackson.
2/Lieut H.L. Houghton.
2/Lieut J.N. Huxter.
2/Lieut J. Birchall.
2/Lieut A.G. Twaddell.

"D" COMPANY.

Captain D. J. Mearns M.C.
Lieut. W. L. Thompson.
2/Lieut W. E. Fowles.
2/Lieut F. T. Robinson.
2/Lieut H. C. Thewlis.
2/Lieut A. Knowles.
2/Lieut Hilton.

OFFICERS DETACHED FOR DUTY.

Lieut. H. West.   172nd Infantry Brigade.
Lieut G. B. Smith.   57th Division.
Captain R.B. Fairclough M.C.   XI Corps Concentration Camp.

2/4th BN. SOUTH LANCASHIRE REGIMENT.

NOMINAL ROLL OF OFFICERS.

Appendix 91.

Commanding Officer.	Captain J.L.Hadfield M.C
A/Adjutant.	Lieut. J.B.Gordon.
Quartermaster.	Q.M. & Lieut. C.A.Lawrence

DETACHED.

Lieut. G.B.Smith.   Attached to R.T.O. Arras.

WAR DIARY or INTELLIGENCE SUMMARY

Army Form C. 2118.

2/4th S. Lanc. Regt.

January 1919

Place	Date	Hour	Summary of Events and Information	Remarks and references to Appendices
MARDEUIL			Battalion employed three days a week on salvage work of arms, other days Educational and General Training	
	4/1/19		2nd Lt J.D. Fitzgerald leave expired 4/12/18, not having returned to France is struck off strength. (Marked on H.S.R. "deserter") 2nd Lt R.J. Haymant M.C. transported to 9th Bn K.L.R. on (Cologne 24/12/18)	R.O.7
	7/1/19		5th John Rambo struck off strength to Bn to XI Corps concentration camp. Capt R.B. Fairclough M.C. to concentration camp struck off strength. R.O.7	R.O.7
	17/1/19		2/Lt A.J. Marsdale, 2/Lt W.E. Touler, Lt W.L. Thompson to Dispersal centre for Demobilisation	R.O.7
	23/1/19		Battn inspected and troops by Divisional commander	R.O.7
	24/1/19		2/Lt D Lewis to Dispersal centre	R.O.6
	27/1/19		2/Lt D. Lewis to dispersal centre for Demobilisation. KING'S COLOUR consecrated by the Assistant Chaplain-General Bishop GWYNNE assisted by Major-Gen K.W.R BARNES CMG, DSO at DUISANS. 2/Lt C.C. EVANS to dispersal centre for Demobilisation.	R.O.6
	31/1/19		C/ Lt R MILBURN to dispersal centre for Demobilisation. Strength of the Battn 31/1/19 12 offrs (including Capt & chaplain attd) plus offrs + numbers at OR leaving and joining the Battn also turned in our secondary lists of other officers. Nominal Roll of Officers.	R.O.6

Appendix C

NOMINAL ROLL OF OFFICERS.

Commanding Officer.	Lieut.Colonel W. McClure.
Second in Command.	Major R. A. Fox M.C.
Battalion Intelligence Officer.	Captain A.T.T. Storey O.B.E.
Demobilization Officer.	Lieut. J. B. Gordon.
A/Adjutant.	Captain C. E. Clarkson.
Quartermaster.	Captain R. A. McWilliam.
Signal Officer.	2/Lieut. J.B.S. Davis.
Asst. Adjutant.	Lieut. A.R. St George.
Transport Officer.	Lieut. A. M. Temple.
Canteen Officer.	Lieut. A. J. Watson.
Medical Officer.	Lieut. G. S. Lambeth M.C. M.R.C. U.S.A.
Chaplain.	Captain J. M. Short C.F. C.E.

"A" COMPANY.

Captain B. Milburn. (Proceeded for demobilization).
Lieut. T. Law.
Lieut. G. Alston M.M.
2/Lieut. D. Lewis (Proceeded for Demobilization).
2/Lieut. R. S. Moss.
2/Lieut. H. A. Roberts.
2/Lieut. C. C. Evans. (Proceeded for Demobilization).
2/Lieut. J. Wilson.

"B" COMPANY.

Captain J. L. Hadfield.
Lieut. H. L. Stevens.
2/Lieut J. F. Nicoll.
2/Lieut. T. Jones.
2/Lieut A.E.W. Beard.
2/Lieut. T.H. Hopkins (Proceeded for Demobilization).

"C" Company.

Lieut. E. W. Hodson.
Lieut. F. I. Jackson.
2/Lieut. A. G. Twaddell (Proceeded for demobilization).
2/Lieut. H. L. Houghton.
2/Lieut. J. N. Huxster.
2/Lieut. J. Birchall.

"D" COMPANY.

Captain D. J. Mearns M.C.
Lieut. W. L. Thompson. (Proceeded for Demobilization).
2/Lieut. J.H.F. Hilton.
2/Lieut. W. E. Fowles (Proceeded for Demobilization).
2/Lieut. H. C. Thewlis.
2/Lieut. F. T. Robinson.
2/Lieut. A. Knowles.

OFFICERS DETACHED FOR DUTY.

Lieut. H. West.	172nd Infantry Brigade.
Lieut. B. B. Smith.	57th Division.
2/Lieut. C.H. Tranter.	57th Division.

Appendix 81

Strength on last return. 42 - 646.

5 Other Ranks		Rejoined from Hospital.	
3 " "		To hospital.	2/1/19.
2 " "		To base for Dispersal Area.	2/1/19.
1 " "		XX XXXXXXXX	XX/XX/XX.
1 " "		To C.C.S.	7/1/19.
2 " "		Rejoined from Hospital.	7/1/19.
4 " "		" " "	4/1/19
7 " "		" " "	9/1/19
1 " "		" " Base.	17/1/19.
8 " "		To hospital	13/1/19.
2 " "		Rejoined from Base.	19/1/19.
1 " "		" " C.C.S.	19/1/19.
1 " "		" " Rouen Milty Prison	24/1/19.
22 " "		To Dispersal centre.	10/1/19.
1 " "		" " "	13/1/19.
40 " "		" " "	14/1/19.
5 " "		" " "	17/1/19.
14 " "		" " "	18/1/19.
3 " "		" " "	19/1/19.
5 " "		" " "	20/1/19.
2 " "		" " "	21/1/19.
30 XXXXXX "		" " "	24/1/19.
1 " "		" " "	25/1/19.
6 " "		" " "	26/1/19.
26 " "		" " "	27/1/19.
3 " "		" " "	28/1/19.
15 " "		" " "	31/1/19.
Captain B Millburn.		" " "	31/1/19.
2/Lt Hopkins T.M.		" " "	31/1/19.
2/Lt Evans C.C.		" " "	27/1/19.
Major R.A.Fox M.C.		Granted 14 Days leave to U.K.	2/1/19.
1 Other Rank		To Mospital	26/1/19.

AWARDS
  No 201326 Sgt (A/CSM) W. Savage.   Awarded D.C.M.
            1181(Authority New Year Honours 1/1/19.)
  No 202225 Pte (L/Cpl) W. Austin.   Awarded M.S.M.
            (Authority New Years Honours 1/1/19.)

3 Other Ranks   To Dispersal Centre.   28/1/19.

WAR DIARY
of
INTELLIGENCE SUMMARY.

(Erase heading not required.)

Army Form C.2118

2/4 S Lanc Regt
Sheet 36.

February.

Place	Date	Hour	Summary of Events and Information	Remarks and references to Appendices
MAROEUIL	1/2/19		2/Lt Y H Hopkins and 10 other Ranks proceeded for Demobilization	RAY
	2/2/19		Capt A. T. T. Storey O.B.E. and 22 other Ranks proceeded for Demobilization.	RAY
	3/2/19		13 other Ranks proceeded for Demobilization.	RAY
	6/2/19		20 other Ranks proceeded for Demobilization.	RAY
	5/2/19		2/Lt J. Birchall proceeded for Demobilization.	RAY
	10/2/19		Lieut J. Alston, Lieut J H F Wilcom, 2/Lt J Jones, 2/Lt J J Nichol, 2/Lt J Shurris, 2/Lt J Wilson and 189 other Ranks proceeded to join 2nd South Lancs Regt.	RAY
	14/2/19		2 other Ranks proceeded for Demobilization.	RAY
	14/2/19		Capt J. L. H. notified awarded M.C. (Immediate Honours) London Gazette. Capt. D. A. Duncan awarded M.C. (Immediate Honours) 15/2/19 2/Lt R.S. Moore 15/2/19	RAY
			2/Lt D. A. Duncan awarded M.C. (Immediate Honours) 15/2/19 2/Lt R.S. Moore 15/2/19	
			20 other Ranks proceeded for Demobilization.	
	19/2/19		2 other Ranks proceeded for Demobilization.	RAY
	20/2/19		2/Lt A. W. Beard, 2/Lt J. N. Hugh, 2/Lt R.S. Moore, 2/Lt H L Hughes and 8 other Ranks proceeded to join 2nd South Lancs Regt. Capt A. R. S. George, Lt A. J. Watson and 20 other Ranks proceeded on Demobilization.	RAY
	21/2/19		R36 other Ranks proceeded on Demobilization.	RAY
	22/2/19		7 Other Ranks proceeded on Demobilization	BL

Army Form C. 2118.

WAR DIARY
or
INTELLIGENCE SUMMARY.
(Erase heading not required.)

Sheet 37

Instructions regarding War Diaries and Intelligence Summaries are contained in F. S. Regs., Part II. and the Staff Manual respectively. Title pages will be prepared in manuscript.

Place	Date	Hour	Summary of Events and Information	Remarks and references to Appendices
MARŒUIL	23/2/19		Maj. R.A. Fox MC and 24 O.Rs. Ranks proceed for demobilisation	65k
"	26/2/19		2.Lt & Capt RA McWilliam & 17 O.Rs Ranks proceed for demobilisation	65k
"	27/2/19		11 O.Rs Ranks proceed for demobilisation	65k
"	28/2/19		1 Offr & Rank proceed for demobilisation	Appendix D1
			Renewed Roll of Officers 28/2/19.	
			Strength of Batt'n 13 officers 101 OR	

William McClure Lt.Col.
Cmdg. 1 Gordons.

2/4th BN SOUTH LANCASHIRE REGIMENT.

Appendix D

NOMINAL ROLL OF OFFICERS.

Commanding Officer.	Lieut. Colonel W. McClure.
Adjutant.	Captain C.E.Clarkson.
Demobilization Officer.	Lieut. J.B.Gordon.
Transport Officer.	Lieut. A.M.Temple.
Quartermaster.	Captain J.L.Hadfield M.C.
Company Commander. "D" Coy.	Captain D.J.Mearns M.C.
Company Commander. "C" Company.	Captain E.W.Hodson.
Education Officer.	2/Lieut. F.T.Robinson.
Second in Command Company.	Lieut. H.L.Stevens.
" " " "	Lieut. F.I.Jackson.
Platoon Commander.	2/Lieut. C.H.Tranter.

DETACHED FOR DUTY.

Lieut. H. West.   172nd Infantry Brigade.
Lieut. G.B.Smith.   Demobilization Officer, 57th Division.

Army Form C. 2118.

WAR DIARY
or
INTELLIGENCE SUMMARY.
(Erase heading not required.)

Sheet 39.

Place	Date	Hour	Summary of Events and Information	Remarks and references to Appendices
MARŒUIL	7/3/19		10 OR proceeded to Dispersal Centre for demobilisation	686
"	14/3/19		Capt H.S. SAWYER proceeded to Dispersal Centre for demobilisation	686
"	18/3/19		5 OR proceeded to Dispersal Centre for demobilisation	686
"	24/3/19		Capt A.M. TEMPLE 2/1 Dorset Yeomanry att. 2/4 S.LR proceed for demobilisation	686
"	25/3/19		Capt. E.W. HODSON 2/4 Capt. TRANTER +19 OR proceed for demobilisation	686
"	26/3/19		5 OR proceeded to join 2nd Bn. S.L.N.R.	686
"	27/3/19		2nd Lt F.T. ROBINSON Lt. F.T. JACKSON proceeded to Dispersal Centre for Demobilisation	686
"	28/3/19		Capt + Lt C.A. LAWRENCE returned from sick leave to Battalion	686
			Strength of Battn. 31/3/19 6 offrs 52 OR	Appendix E.

Monthly Roll of Officer

Vivian W. Blue.

LIEUT.-COLONEL,
COMMANDING,
2/4th BN. SOUTH LANCASHIRE REGIMENT.

2/4th BN SOUTH LANCASHIRE REGIMENT.

NOMINAL ROLL OF OFFICERS.

Commanding Officer.	Lieut. Colonel W. McClure.
Adjutant.	Captain C.E.Clarkson.
Lewis Gun Officer.	Captain J.L.Hadfield M.C.
Demobilization Officer.	Lieut. J. B. Gordon.
O.C. "D" Company.	Captain D. J. Mearns M.C.
2nd in Command.	Lieut. H. L. Stevens.
Quartermaster.	Q.M. & Lieut. C.A.Lawrence.

DETACHED FOR DUTY.

Lieut. G. B. Smith.	Demobilization Officer, 57th Division.

2/4 E Lanc R Army Form C. 2118.

WAR DIARY
or
INTELLIGENCE SUMMARY.
(Erase heading not required.)

Sheet 39.

Place	Date	Hour	Summary of Events and Information	Remarks and references to Appendices
Brig HQ MANDEVIL	31/4/19		LT. A.L. STEVENS + 1.OR proceed for demobilisation	CCC
"	30/4/19		LT. COL. W McCLURE + 1.OR proceed for demobilisation	CCC
			Strength of Battn 30/4/19 6 officers 52.OR	CCC
			Nominal Roll of officers	Appendix F1 & F2

Stevens
Captain
for Commanding
2/4 L South Lancashire Regt.

Appendix F1

2/4th BN SOUTH LANCASHIRE REGIMENT.

NOMINAL ROLL OF OFFICERS.

Commanding Officer.	Captain J. L. Hadfield M.C.
Adjutant.	Captain C. E. Clarkson.
Quartermaster.	Q.M. & Lieut. C.A. Lawrence.
Company Commander.	Captain D. J. Mearns M.C.
Demobilization Officer.	Lieut. J. B. Gordon.

OFFICER DETACHED FOR DUTY.

Lieut. G.B. Smith.   Attached to R.T.O. Arras.

From:- O.C.
　　　　2/4th Battn SouthbLancashire Regt

To:- HeadQuarters,
　　　　172 Infantry Brigade.

A4/259.

　　　　　　　Herewith War Diary for the month of May.

　　　　　　　　　　　　　　　　　　[signature]
　　　　　　　　　　　　　　　　　　Captain,
　　　　　　　　　　　　　　Commanding,
31/5/1919.　　　　　　　　2/4th Battn South Lancashire Regt

2/4th BN. SOUTH LANCASHIRE REGIMENT. WAR DIARY or INTELLIGENCE SUMMARY.

Army Form C. 2118.

2/4 S Lanc R
Sheet 4 of 4 / 5 / 28

MAY 1919.

Place	Date	Hour	Summary of Events and Information	Remarks and references to Appendices
Tournai	13/5/19		14 OR proceeded to 2nd Batt. South Lancashire Regt.	WD
"	14/5/19		Capt. R. Murrell M.C. } Proceed for demobilization Capt Chas E Clarkson }	WD
"	31/5/19		Strength of Battalion 4 officers 37 OR.	WD
			Nominal role of officers	9. APPENDIX

J. J. Hardwick
Capt.
Commanding
2/4 South Lancashire Regt.

57TH DIVISION
172ND. INFY BDE

2-5TH BN STH LANCS REGT
1915 SEP — 1916 FEB
AND FEB — ~~NOV~~ DEC 1917

DISBANDED FEB 18

www.ingramcontent.com/pod-product-compliance
Lightning Source LLC
Chambersburg PA
CBHW081421160426
43193CB00013B/2165